**"Sexually,
I'm more of a
Switzerland"**

David Rose lives
in New York.

Also by David Rose

They call me naughty Lola:
Personal ads from the *London Review of Books*

"Sexually, I'm more of a Switzerland"

Personal ads from the
London Review of Books

Edited and with an
Introduction by David Rose

PICADOR

First published 2010 by Scribner, a division of Simon & Schuster, Inc., New York

First published in Great Britain 2010 by Picador

First published in paperback 2011 by Picador
an imprint of Pan Macmillan, a division of Macmillan Publishers Limited
Pan Macmillan, 20 New Wharf Road, London N1 9RR
Basingstoke and Oxford
Associated companies throughout the world
www.panmacmillan.com

ISBN 978-0-330-51900-7

9 8 7 6 5 4 3 2 1

A CIP catalogue record for this book is available from
the British Library.

Typeset in Quadraat by Andrew Barker Information Design
Printed and bound by CPI Group (UK) Ltd, Croydon, CR0 4YY

This book is dedicated
to the memory of
Robert Craig 'Evel' Knievel
and Bridget Anne Rose.

Also all the
assistant managers at
Copperas Hill post office.

And Elvis.

Luasc anuas a charbaid,
Stad agus tabhair geábh dom.
TCB.

Contents

"Sexually, I'm more of a Switzerland"

Introduction

My mother always hoped I'd apply for a job at Copperas Hill post office. In November 1990 she was especially enthusiastic about it because things had been hotting up between Saddam Hussein and the Kuwaitis and a war at Christmas is always great news for postal delivery services. She was convinced that if I played my cards right, I could make assistant manager one day.

Naturally, every other Thursday for the past eleven years – copy deadline day for *London Review of Books* personals advertisers – I've wondered where I might be now had I bothered filling in that application form. Not working at Copperas Hill post office, that's for sure; they had wild-cat strikes and massive lay-offs towards the end of the nineties. But as my life meandered away from fighting the home front against Saddam, only a wizard could have anticipated that I'd spend the most fruitful years of my life agonizing over word-counts with soup-perverts:

I put the phrase 'five-header bi-sexual orgy' in this ad to increase my Google hits. Really I'm looking for someone who likes hearty soups and jigsaws of kittens. Woman, 62. Berwick. Box no. 7862.

Of course, I would never have become the angst-devouring love-conduit through which Britain's most romantically awkward eggheads play out their weird and frequently disturbing sex rituals. Life would be much duller, although I'd have fewer bad dreams and wouldn't have to shower quite so often.

An ancient Czech legend says that any usurper who places the Crown of Saint Wenceslas on his head is doomed to die within a year. During

World War II, Reinhard Heydrich, the Nazi governor of the puppet Protectorate of Bohemia and Moravia, secretly wore the crown believing himself to be a great king. He was assassinated less than a year later by the Czech resistance. I have many more stories like this one. I will tell you them all and we will make love. Man, 47. Box no. 6889.

Since the LRB personals began in October 1998, I've dealt with the phone calls, emails, letters, faxes and – always less welcome – occasional personal visits from within a very incongruous set-up. While the offices of the magazine have remained very firmly in Bloomsbury, the nerve-centre of the personals section was, for the most part, a water-logged shed in Liverpool. Really it was the back of an illegally built garage, but we'll call it a shed because no motor vehicle ever went in there and its main function was the storage of rusted Woolworth's power tools, an assortment of lawn-patching compounds and my (now deceased) mother's oxygen cylinders (she had dodgy lungs and we kept these in case we ever needed to re-inflate her).

When it rained, the uninsulated corrugated roof made it sound like a clown was firing a machine-gun at a sad robot. There was a power supply that was so precarious I once got an electric shock eating a trifle. And in the corner lived a nest of badgers. Before that the personals were managed from a flat above a bankrupt florist south of the Thames. Recently it's been in a Brooklyn office shared with a very serious publishing outfit who never reciprocate a round of drinks, hardly ever say hello and rarely smile unless someone has made a very hilarious remark about Adorno. Which happened only once and it wasn't very hilarious.

When someone asks my advice about what to include or exclude in their personal advert, these have been the common conditions under which I've responded – noise, damp, Adorno, badgers. Truthfully, had I worked in surroundings befitting a

Zurich-based insurance company, I couldn't have offered
any better advice. I was once asked by the Jewish Community
Centre for London to be part of a panel discussion about dating.
I'm not Jewish, which surprised everyone, but also I know
absolutely nothing about dating. Those early phone calls I
received from potential advertisers, full of typical British
insecurity and self-deprecation – people worried that all they
could say about them-selves was that they had exceptional liver
function and knew from years of looking after their ageing
parents how to keep a glass eye sterile – seemed good enough
to me. I mean, I *liked* these people. They were fun to talk to;
painfully honest but also engaging, witty and clever. Why not
just throw it all out there? At the time I'd been working at the
magazine for less than a year, and working in advertising for
just a little longer. Not at the rock 'n' roll creative end of things,
but in sales – selling space in car magazines before I moved to
the London Review. People asked my advice as if I knew what I
was talking about – as if, rather than working in ad sales, I was a
relationship counsellor. It didn't matter when I'd explain I was
just a very junior sales guy, these people innocently trusted me
and every enquiry would end with 'What do you think?' or 'Do I
sound like an idiot?' or 'I'm not sure I should make it read like
I'm a serial killer':

Everyone. My life is a mind-numbing cesspit of despair and self-
loathing. Just fuck off. Or else write back and we'll make love.
Gentleman, 37. Box no. 5369.

All I could ever tell anyone was, 'It's great, just do it.' Partly out of
my own English awkwardness, partly out of a fear of not making
the sale back when my targets were impossible and I had no
clients, but mostly out of sincerely getting a kick from what they'd
written. This wasn't how other lonely hearts columns operated.

On a flight from Glasgow about a year after the column began, where I'd been on a BBC daytime show about lonely hearts with a rogue's gallery of dating experts, advice columnists, and women's magazine psychologists, I gave a copy of the LRB ads to a woman who ran an agency that produced the personals sections of many broadsheet newspapers. Other publications tend to contract out their personals sections to specialist dating firms rather than ad-sales companies. Usually people phone a premium-rate number and they're asked pseudo-psychoanalytic questions such as 'With which historical figure do you most identify?' or, 'If you were part of a celebrity coupling, who would be your ideal partner?' The answers are then translated into a personal ad. In occasional attempts to be more professional I've tried this approach on LRB advertisers, but with less than encouraging results:

I am more like Grand Duke Nicholas Mikhailovich of Russia than anyone else who has ever advertised here. Man, 54. Box no. 5349.

You're Helen Mirren. I'm Will Self. One half of this century's über-couple-to-be seeks tousled fems to 50 for weekends full of recondite wines, obscure blandishments, and winning references to abstruse 11th century sexual practices. No loons. Box no. 7936.

The personals sections managed by this particular agency were full of gorgeous, healthy, intelligent people. Each presented a paradigm of human excellence, albeit infused with a somewhat eerie sense of eugenic urgency. Naturally, she was appalled by the LRB ads. 'These are awful,' she said, 'you can't let people say these things about themselves,' and then she offered to take over running the section.

I've grown used to this kind of response, but it's still exasperating. Even if the advertisers in other columns haven't been coerced into a clumsy rhetorical liposuction of all the junk of their lives and were genuinely Nietzschean Übermenschen (notwithstanding their appearance in – sotto voce – a lonely hearts column), the existence of such characterless people can only be depressing for the vast majority of us jaded, cynical, out-of-sync-with-the-world types:

I hate you all. I hate London. I hate books. I hate critics. I hate this magazine, I hate this column and I hate all the goons who appear in it. But if you have large breasts, are younger than 30 and don't want to talk about the novel you're 'writing' I'll put all that aside for approximately two hours one Saturday afternoon in January. Man, 33. Box no. 7810.

Of course, there's no need to feel intimidated by the shining beauties occasionally sprinkled across small-ads sections like glitter on a dog turd. Significantly, one of the most revealing and often unquoted statistics about personal ads is that the commonest complaints are to do with advertisers rarely being the way they describe themselves in their ads. Such instances of advertisers not being altogether candid – or, more accurately, lying – are probably the cumulative results of dating-agency spin, being delusional about their sense of self or simply a fear of not being interesting enough. It's not a complaint we get at the LRB. Although we have occasionally had concerned phone calls from respondents surprised that certain adverts weren't, after all, intended ironically –

My hobbies include crying and hating men. F, 29. Box no. 8620.

I'm not convinced personal ads tell us anything about human behaviour other than that our ideas of what makes us attractive to others are based on very arbitrary assumptions. Speedos aren't a good look for anyone. Knowledge of circuit training and which protein shake is best for a post-squat-thrust warm-down isn't going to win you points in the 'great to talk to' league. In this sense, the personal ads in the *London Review of Books* are very liberating. Their strength comes from resoundingly rejecting those archetypal elements of attraction that press so heavily on our insecurities but that few of us actually possess. Bespectacled and melanin-deprived, the LRB personals tell us not to be ashamed; to relax a little and enjoy what's out there without feeling threatened by it. We can read them without ever having to suck in our gut:

Young, charming, thoughtful, attractive, sporty, zesty, intelligent. None of these are me, but if you'd like to spend an afternoon or more considering alternative adjectives to be applied to 53-year-old cantankerous dipshit, write now to box no. 0927.

After all these years I'm honestly still cheered by the phone calls I get from people as insecure about their attractiveness as I am. I enjoy talking to these people – rich, lively, and (it's true) often strange folk whose main selling point is their knowledge of medieval filigree, or their jam collections, or their fondness for ingesting things they probably shouldn't be ingesting:

They say you are what you eat. I'm eight Panadols, a few daily Seroxats, a couple of Senokots, a whole clutch of Nuvelles and – since I came around this afternoon – three crayons and a Maxi Pad. Dizzy historian (M, 54) seeks woman for whom the terms 'good times', 'tracking device' and 'A&E' aren't always a million miles away from each other. Box no. 3235.

Perhaps we're all taken in by the Scheherazade effect – a term coined by evolutionary psychologist Geoffrey Miller* in

---

* G. F. Miller, *The Mating Mind: How Sexual Choice Shaped the Evolution of Human Nature*, Heinemann, 2000.

reference to the ancient Persian queen and storyteller of *One Thousand and One Nights*. Like King Shahryar, beheading his virgin brides once he's had his way with them, we read personal ads ready to laugh at them and brush them aside. But, just as Scheherazade permanently stays her execution and wins the affection of her king with tales full of history and humour, so the LRB personals keep us compelled with their inventiveness – their minute performances – engaging us in such a way as to keep us wanting more and thus forever postponing their dismissal:

If you're reading this hoping for a mini-biopic about battles with drugs, cancer and divorce, talk to the guy above. But if you want to know about historical battle sites in Scotland, talk to me. Alan, 45. Scottish historical battle expert and BDSM fetishist. Box no. 8553.

Each advert, whatever first appearances may suggest, is very carefully crafted, often involving hours of pain and self-examination and, very possibly, home-made benzodiazepines:

Yesterday I was a disgusting spectacle in end-stage alcoholism with a gambling problem and not a hope in the world. Today I am the author of this magnificent life-altering statement of yearning and desire. You are a woman to 55 with plenty of cash and very little self-respect. When you reply to this advert your life will never be the same again. My name is Bernard. Never call me Bernie. Box no. 3916.

Despite the number of exchanges between an advertiser and me, it's very rare that I find out if an ad has worked. Although I've heard a handful of success stories, people are very shy about admitting they met their partner through a lonely heart. More often I only hear from the advertiser again if it's to complain about the standard of response generated – the orthodontist who collected cavity samples and proudly sent a whole album's worth of photographs, the woman who posted photocopied passages from the Bible with the cryptic annotation 'I've done this and enjoyed it', or the gentleman whose hobby was documenting his sightings of albino people. This volume, along with the first, *They Call Me Naughty Lola*, merely collects the adverts themselves, but imagine how enlightening (and terrifying) a volume of responses would be.

This advert formally ends the period of my life I like to jokingly refer to as 'the years I spent a lot of money on drugs' and begins the phase I hope will be known in the very near future as 'the weekend I had sex with that guy'. Woman, 32. Box no. 9830.

Even the mode of response is, in itself, an important consideration here because most LRB ads don't give email addresses. They rely, rather, on a box number forwarding system that costs an extra fiver per ad and is entirely at the mercy of the ambiva-lent British postal service and the LRB advertising department's staff holiday schedule:

If fate brings us together, destiny will probably tear us apart. Kismet may see us off in the morning. Causality might cook dinner. Hubris will almost certainly iron my trousers. Determinedly deterministic man, 37. Mostly leaving everything in the hands of Royal Mail and a box number reply-forwarding system that made no sense whatsoever when Louisa at the LRB tried to explain it. Box no. 8522.

Indeed, it may seem to the casual reader that the LRB personals began at the wrong time, coming as they did four years after the birth of one of the most successful online dating communities, Match.com. In this digital generation of social networking sites, the personals in the *London Review of Books* are something of an enigma. Not only have they survived, undiminished in their openness and brutal self-analysis, but they have steadfastly resisted the anodyne resources of the modern dating landscape, as if Match.com, Craigslist and JDate are, if anything, simply too easy, like finding the teacher's edition of the algebra textbook complete with answers in the back.

We make no apologies. The effort of writing and posting a response has always been regarded by our advertisers as an essential part of their vetting procedure. Maybe that's to be expected of a very literary readership. Rather than create a single, generic email that can be sent to as many people as one likes – as is the case on dating websites – respondents to LRB personals have to be much more conscientious. They must choose their stationery carefully, for instance. Would-be Henry Millers could be undone by a coarse sheet of foolscap whilst a self-gummed Avery standard could very easily scupper any advance made by a latter-day Anaïs Nin. Sentences must be beautifully composed and written with a fine calligraphic hand. Every cursive stroke is open to analysis. Every looped 'g' scrutinized for meaning. These are all elements digital dating doesn't allow. Plus, with a written letter, it's impossible to disguise a prison post-mark:

Part biopic, part utopian vision, all epic of redemption amidst the trials of mankind. This personal ad has everything. Woman, 38. Only one conviction for nuisance calling. Box no. 6544.

In the age of Facebook triteness, the ability to engage with even the most fractional components of writing has become an increasingly valuable commodity for any intellectually-minded mate. Shortage, it is true, drives demand:

Dear LRB, I have no money. Please run my advert for free. I want a woman who is 38. Let her know I'm really clever and good-looking. Thanks. Box no. 4487.

But it would be a mistake to assume that our advertisers are simply old-fashioned, or that, as traditional lonely hearts sections become transplanted onto the Internet, the LRB personals column is nothing more than the last tooth in a gum of long-since-vanished small-ads sections. Perhaps they are a canon in their own right, presenting a very specific style of writing that is quite apart even from other publications' personal-ads sections. Like haiku or sonnets, they suggest specific constraints of form and metre – a 'house style', if you will – but traverse these frequently with gamesmanship and a desire always to be distinct:

Straight line. Straight line. Funny line. Sucker punch. Busy man, 36. Box no. 9732.

Nor would it be entirely egregious to suggest that they have a small place in the broad aesthetic of British emotional awkwardness that would include Morrissey, Alan Bennett and Philip Larkin at the top of the tree, and my auntie Alice at the root ('I can't dance tonight, lad, me dollypegs are 'urtin'). For LRB readers, the personal ads aren't *cris de coeur* as much as they are bucolic tests of wit and audacity – *poissons d'avril* pinned to the back of the unsuspecting literary establishment. And yet, when all's said and done, they *are* personal ads. They may punch above their weight, but there is an end to them that stops considerably short of art's high table. Their purpose is to attract attention, nothing more. Their absurdity and humour aren't disguises for some deeper intent. They are simple and genuine statements about the people who write them and the people they hope to find. True, their honesty subverts the traditional lonely heart form, and we're often surprised, delighted, or infuriated by their unwavering and messy emotion, inelegantly sprayed across the page like water from a garden hose loose on its faucet, but if an advert doesn't garner a positive response – however entertaining it may be – its author will always consider it a failure. Whilst the stakes aren't necessarily high in the LRB personals, there is always a sense of consequence:

I celebrated my fortieth birthday last week by cataloguing my collection of bird feeders. Next year I'm hoping for sexual intercourse. And a cake. Join my invite mailing list at box no. 6831. Man.

Note for readers: It should be pointed out that the adverts in this volume are no longer active and as such responses cannot be forwarded on to advertisers.

"A shoddily-painted bust of Richard Dudgeon"

What kind of animal are you? I'm a giraffe. No! Wait! I'm a monkey! Welcome to my tree-top paradise. (F, 62). Box no. 0220.

My way or the highway – the two are very often the same with asphalting loon, 53, mixing his own bitumen and coarse aggregate surfacing solutions at box no. 6737.

My success as a lover is matched only by my success in the field of astronomy. Man, 37. WLTM woman to 40 with eyes as big and as bright as those stars that come up over by the trees opposite my house at about 9pm every night, then every 15 minutes or so. You know the ones. I call them the Regular Magic Tree Stars. They may be comets. Or planes. Whatever. Write, we'll have sex, you'll love it. Box no. 8909.

Are you the man of my dreams? Green, 9'10", three eyes, six tentacled arms and reciting the third canto of Edmund Spenser's *The Faerie Queene*[1] whilst crushing football-sized grapes with hoofed feet? Either stop it now or kiss me, you monstrous wine-making fool. Woman, 41, Exeter. Box no. 1011.

The origin of evil may have been a problem for the Romantics, but not for me – I lay it squarely at the door of freeze-dried onions. Come hang perilously on the cliff of soak-before-eating foodstuffs. Conversation is limited,

1 Allegorical epic poem first published in 1590 and written in praise of Queen Elizabeth I. It was published as six books in 1596 (having originally been published as three), with each being an exploration of different virtues. The third book is an examination of chastity.

but the nutritional value is off the meter.[2] Man, 41. Box no. 0524.

....

Gun for hire. Also terrapins for sale. Confused but fully-booked Bradford cowboy-cum-terrarium zoo gardener, WLTM quick-fire Calamity Jane[3] to 50 with no small amount of expertise in rearing amphibious reptiles. Whip-crack-away at box no. 1006.

....

I made this magazine what it is today – a crumbling, shoddily-painted bust of Richard Dudgeon,[4] inventor of the hydraulic jack. Papier mâché-obsessed idiot (M, 42). Box no. 1312.

....

Re-enact the American Civil War[5] in my kitchen. Man, 51, holed up in the larder, seeks Confederate woman for pitched battles with muskets, pikes, and Tefal griddle pans. Must know how to slaughter a perfectly good omelette. Bucks. Box no. 0764.

....

Quornbaya, my Lord, quornbaya. Gay, non-smoking vegetarian Joan Baez fantasist (F, 54). WLTM similar to 60 for textured mycoprotein-based protest music

....

2   100 grams of onions typically contain 12 per cent RDA of vitamin C.

3   Calamity Jane (1852–1903) – born Martha Jane Cannary Burke. North American frontierswoman and the eponymous heroine of the 1953 Warner Bros. musical starring Doris Day.

4   Richard Dudgeon – born in Scotland in 1819. Emigrated to the United States in his youth, where he took a job at the Allaire Iron Works in New York City. He established his own machine shop in 1849 and achieved industrial fame with his portable hydraulic jack (patented in 1851). Prior to the hydraulic jack, the less efficient screw jack was the prevalent lifting device.

5   1861–65.

shenanigans.[6] Someone's cooking meat substitute fajitas, my Lord, quornbaya at box no. 6587.

....

This wheel's on fire.[7] So is my hair. And my under-paid assistant. Beatnik chemist and perennial misfiring love jerk (M, 35) WLTM woman to 40 with asbestos suit and no small knowledge of acids and which things from my bathroom cupboard I shouldn't be mixing them with. Box no. 6190.

....

Man, 41. Not the sharpest sandwich at the picnic. Box no. 2442.

....

A lot of people say these ads are tacky and tasteless.
Not me, and I promise you I know art when I see it. Velvet Elvis and Genuine Pope-shaped hip-flask salesman, 49, looking for woman with lounge bar in the shape of a ship's hull. Anchors away, momma, and bless you, my child. Box no. 1013.

....

One-time Mario Andretti of popular short-lived quad protests seeks Stirling Moss of resurgent leftist agit-prop theatre for nights of frequent pit-stops and dragging up behind the safety car.[8] Must have large bosoms. M, 61. Box no. 8699.

....

6   Quorn is a brand of mycoprotein-based foodstuffs made from the soil mould *Fusarium venenatum* strain PTA-2684. Currently it is the leading brand of vegetarian meat-replacement food in the UK. Joan Baez (b. 1941) – folk singer known for addressing topical and social issues with her music.

7   'This Wheel's on Fire' – written by Bob Dylan and Rick Danko. Performed by Julie Driscoll, Brian Auger, and The Trinity (1968, Marmalade Records). It reached number five in the UK charts. Also recorded by Bob Dylan on his album *The Basement Tapes* (1975, Columbia), and The Band's *Music from Big Pink* (1968, Capitol). Siouxsie and the Banshees recorded a version on their album *Through the Looking Glass* (1987, Polydor).

8   Mario Gabriel Andretti (b. 1940) – Italian-American racing driver. Sir Stirling Craufurd Moss OBE (b. 1929) – retired English racing driver.

"Mentally, I'm a size eight"

If intense, post-fight sex scares you, I'm not the woman for you (amateur big-boned cage wrestler, 62). Box no. 8744.

The low-resolution personal ad. When viewed from a distance it looks amazing, but up close it's pretty poor. Man, 35, Gwent. Box no. 7863.

Nothing says 'I love you' in a more sincere way than being woken with champagne and pastries and roses. Apart from a dog with peanut butter on the roof of his mouth. Write, we'll meet, sleep together and – in the morning, just before my friend's wife tells me to get off their sofa and get out of their house – I'll show you Winston's trick. It's hilarious. You'll have to bring the peanut butter though – they've put locks on all the kitchen cupboards. Man, 26. Box no. 6433.

My last seven adverts in this column were influenced by the early catalogue of Krautrock band, Paternoster. This one, however, is based entirely around the work of Gil Scott-Heron. Man, 32. Possibly the last person you want to be stood next to at a house-party you've been dragged along to by a friend who wants to get off with the flatmate of the guy whose birthday it is. Hey! Have you ever heard Boards of Canada? They're amazing; I'll burn you a CD.[9] Box no. 3178.

9 Paternoster – progressive Austrian Krautrock band largely unknown beyond circles of Krautrock enthusiasts. They realized one (self-titled) album in 1972 (Ohrwaschl Records). Gil Scott-Heron – American poet and musician considered one of the earliest pioneers of political rap music and best known for the poem and song 'The Revolution Will Not Be Televised'. Boards of Canada – one of the musical projects of Scottish brothers Michael Sandison

This advert is about as close as I come to meaningful interaction with other adults. Woman, 51. Not good at parties but tremendous breasts. Box no. 5436.

Years of cigarette smoke can put one hell of a patina on a guy's complexion. F with hot soapy water, coarse brush and a poor sense of smell/sobriety required by jug-faced M, 57. Box no. 4674.

I'm no Victoria's Secret model.[10] Man, 62. Box no. 3280.

Meet the new face of indoor bowling! More or less the same as the old face, but less facial hair and better teeth. M, 28. Box no. 3377.

I cannot guarantee you'll fall in love with me, but I can promise you the best home-brewed beetroot wine you'll have ever tasted. Now if that doesn't sound like a fermented bucket of yummy siphoned lustiness I just don't know what does. Man, 41. Stupid like wow! Box no. 9851.

It is my manifest destiny to find a man through this column and marry him. Woman, 103. Box no. 2134.

The celebrity I resemble the most is Potsie from *Happy Days*. What feels so right can't be wrong. Man, 46.[11] Box no. 2480.

---

and Marcus Eoin. The name is taken from the National Film Board of Canada (see p. 41, n. 34).

10 US retailer of women's lingerie.

11 *Happy Days* – US sitcom that ran from 1974 until 1984. The show was set in the 1950s and 1960s and centred on the Cunningham family of Milwaukee. A supporting character, Warren 'Potsie' Weber, was one of the few characters to run the entire course of the series and was played by Anson Williams, second cousin of Dr Henry Heimlich, known for the Heimlich Manoeuvre for treating

Mentally, I'm a size eight. Compulsive-eating F, 52, WLTM man to 25 for whom the phrase 'beauty is only skin-deep' is both a lifestyle choice and a religious ethos. Box no. 5115.

I've been parachuted in to return this column to its usual standard. Man, 96. Box no. 3270.

Drooling, toothless sociopath (M, 57) seeks F any age to help make this abandoned gas station kiosk feel more like home. Must bring shoes (size 10). Box no. 5310.

Tall, handsome, well-built, articulate, intelligent, sensitive, yet often grossly inaccurate man, 21. Cynics (and some cheap Brentwood psychiatrists) may say 'pathological liar', but I like to use 'creative with reality'. Join me in my 36-bedroomed mansion on my Gloucestershire estate, set in 400 acres of wild-stag populated woodland. East Ham.[12] Box no. 0620.

Time is the serenest beauty of the camp, but only I have the reflexes of a fox. And a badger's sense of smell. Woman. 51. Box no. 0522.

I vacillate wildly between a number of archetypes including, but not limited to, Muriel Spark witticism-trading doyenne, Mariella Frostrup charismatic socialite, brooding, intense Marianne Faithfull visionary, and kleptomaniac Germaine Greer amateur upholsterer and

choking victims. The show's theme tune (composed by Charles Fox and Norman Gimbel) included the line 'Feels so right, it can't be wrong'.

12 East Ham is a built-up urban district in the London Borough of Newham and not, in fact, in Gloucestershire.

ladies' league darts champion.[13] Woman, 43. Everything I just said was a lie. Apart from the bit about darts. And kleptomania. Great tits though. Box no. 2236.

Rippling hunk of a guy; washboard stomach, blonde, blue-eyed, not quite 50, WLTM woman with open mind and some experience of hallucinogens. Box no. 4532.

Two out of every ten times I'm absolutely correct. Man, 35 (Islington). Non-smoker, academic, caring, solvent, passionate, articulate, full head of hair. Box no. 7326.

Just as chugging on a bottle of White Lightning[14] on a park bench will make you nauseous and diminish the respect of your peers, yet taking just a glass of cold cider on a balmy summer evening will quench your thirst and take you back to heady days frolicking in West Country apple orchards, so it is with this ad. Man, 37. Refreshing in small sips where the delicate nuances of Somerset burst through full and flavoursome, but anything bigger and you'll end up puking over your own shoes and smelling of wee. Box no. 8930.

My advert comes in the form of interpretive dance. Man, 62. Box no. 4458.

---

13 Muriel Spark (1918–2006) – Scottish novelist whose works include *The Prime of Miss Jean Brodie*. Mariella Frostrup (b. 1962) – television presenter, panelist, and critic. Germaine Greer (b. 1939) – Australian writer, scholar, critic, and author of the 1970 international best-seller *The Female Eunuch*.

14 White Lightning – fermented corn syrup marketed as cider by brewers Scottish Courage. Synonymous with British hooligan youth culture and vagrant street-drinking in the early 2000s due to its low price, wide availability, and high alcohol concentration (7.5 per cent alcohol by volume).

I'm the entire third chapter from that shite book they compiled from these ads.[15] Go figure. Man, 57. Box no. 0733.

Sent to prison by a military court for a crime he didn't commit, this man (32) promptly escaped from a maximum security stockade into the Los Angeles underground. Today, still wanted by the government, he survives as a soldier of fortune. If you have a problem – if no one else can help – and if you can find him – maybe you can fall in love with irritating TV trivia genius, wearing white socks regardless of the colour of his trousers.[16] Box no. 0533.

Sweet Caroline (da, da, daaa) – good times never felt so good. Man, 42 – bouncy and irritating like a bad tune you can't get out of your head. Come on, Silver Lady, take my hand – I won't walk out on you again, believe me. Thank your lucky stars at box no. 0618 that we're not as smart as we like to think we are. Cambs.[17]

At first glance you may consider me a true modernist in the von Webern sense, but – like him – deep down I'm

15   *They Call Me Naughty Lola*, a collection of personal adverts from the *London Review of Books*. Published in 2006 by Profile in the UK and Scribner in the US. The third chapter was called 'Last time I had this much fun, I was on forty tablets a day'.

16   The advert references the opening sequence of NBC TV series *The A-Team*, which ran for five seasons between 1983 and 1987.

17   'Sweet Caroline' – written and performed by Neil Diamond and taken from the album *Sweet Caroline* (1969, UNI/MCA). It reached number four in the Billboard charts. 'Silver Lady' – written by Tony Macaulay and Geoff Stephens and performed by David Soul on his album *Playing to an Audience of One* (1977, Private Stock Records). The song reached number one in the UK singles chart. 'Lucky Stars' – written by Dean Friedman and performed by Friedman and Denise Marsa. Taken from the album *"Well, Well", Said The Rocking Chair* (1978, Lifesong). Reached number three in the UK charts.

very much a romantic.[18] As my collection of taxidermied amphibians will testify. Man, 60. Box no. 9444.

....

Why waste time in the bath? M, 45, with secret to natural, water-free cleanliness – psychic showering, bathe in your own karma (patent pending). Seeks woman to 50 for invigorating wash-down in the fountain of the mind. Must be prepared to lose friends and never be allowed in restaurants again. Box no. 0217.

....

Man, 42. WLTM woman to 50 to help harness the disappointment I routinely create in all my relationships. Own tap shoes an advantage. Box no. 3868.

....

Being a Capricorn with an ascendant Sagittarius, I only ever date women in February when my moon is in the seventh house. If you're a Virgo with Leo or Aries rising, or Taurus with Pisces or Gemini rising, or Cancer with an Aquarian moon, or Libra with a cousin called Derek, or Scorpio with a dachshund, write now to Sunday newspaper columnist and conjurer (M, 53), fast running out of excuses as to why he hasn't had sex in over three years. Strictly no women with a fear of cats. Or a reluctance to participate in pagan rejuvenation rites involving the drinking of our own urine. Box no. 9783.

....

'Go on, son, hit me in the stomach'. Everybody's boring uncle, 51 ('and I got this scar in Korea'). Box no. 0534.

....

18   Anton von Webern (1883–1945) – Austrian composer and conductor and a member of the Second Viennese School. He was accidentally shot and killed by a US soldier on 15 September 1945.

"The usual hyperbole and a whiff of playful narcissism"

In my house the electric sander is king and I am its willing knave. The toaster is chancellor. You (woman to 37, Cambs. and surrounding) can be a scullery maid. My palmtop is queen. Obey its organisational mastery and megapixel display properties at box no. 5712.

I have a mug that says 'World's Greatest Lover'. I think that's my referees covered. How about you? Man. 37. Bishopsgate. Box no. 8763.

Brief personality multi-choice: you're reading a respected literary magazine when you see an advert from an American, intelligent, 57-year-old man with his own computing business and really impressive motorbike. He is obviously the man of your dreams. Do you a) cancel your subscription and start reading *Hello!*, b) sulk in bed, wishing you were a woman, c) join the queue and write to box no. 2545?

I will file you under 'T' for 'Totty'. Just after 'T' for 'Teutonic' and before 'T' for 'Tributary'. You can file me under 'P' for 'Pithy'. And my shoes under 'R' for 'Recherché'. Well-turned-out man, 46. Box no. 7892.

Philanthropy is my middle name. It's just a name though so don't be expecting any free rides. You can call me Mr Wallace. My first name is none of your business. Applications to box no. 9741.

We've all made mistakes. Mine was a cerise pump during London Fashion Week 2004. Style troubadour (M, 35). WLTM similar, or appropriately dour fag hag. Box no. 8643.

All humans are 99.9% genetically identical, so don't even think of ending any potential relationship begun here with 'I just don't think we have enough in common'.[19] Science has long since proven that I am the man for you (41, likes to be referred to as 'Wing Commander' in the bedroom). Box no. 3501.

Normally on the first few dates I borrow mannerisms from the more interesting people I know and very often steal phrases and anecdotes from them along with concepts and ideas from obscure yet wittily-written books. It makes me appear more attractive and personable than I actually am. With you, however, I'm going to be a belligerent old shit from the very beginning. That's because I like you and feel ready to give you honesty. Belligerent old shit (M, 53). Box no. 6378.

Whilst I look forward to an engaging and fulfilling relationship with someone whose emotional needs dovetail neatly with my own in a way that enables us both to express ourselves freely and exist together with mutual respect and compassion, I see absolutely no harm whatsoever in having wild, disgusting, nasty one-off sex with just about anyone. That's where you come in – woman to whatever age from anywhere either within or from outside the M25 with a pulse and four hours to spare. Exquisite breasts and own Oyster card[20] a distinct advantage. Man, 34. Box no. 2582.

19   Research figure published by Celera Genomics in 2001. The figure was disputed in 2004 by a team from Cold Spring Harbor Laboratory in New York and by Stephen W. Scherer, et al., in the results of a study published in the magazine *Nature Genetics*, putting similarities at between 99.7 per cent and 99.8 per cent. President Bill Clinton used the statistic in a speech in 2000, stating 'All human beings, regardless of race, are more than 99.9 per cent the same'.

20   Electronic ticketing system used on London-based transport networks.

If clumsy, unfeeling lust is your bag, write to the ad
above. Otherwise write to me, mid-forties M with boy next
door looks, man from U.N.C.L.E. charm, and Fresh Prince
of Bel-Air casual insouciance . Wicky wicky wick yo.[21] Box
no. 2851.

I have accommodated many terms from the world of
embroidery into my bedroom lexicon. Whenever we make
love, you will be sexually satisfied whilst also subliminally
studying an accredited course in a skill long lost to women
over the ages. Man (57): lover, instructor, and, providing
you have gained enough modular credits throughout the
term, invigilator on your final exam. Box no. 3721.

The usual hyperbole infuses this ad with a whiff of playful
narcissism and Falstaffian bathos. But scratch below the
surface and you'll soon find that I really am the greatest
man ever to have lived. Truly great man, 37. Better than
Elvis and Ghandi. You'll never be a genuinely worthy
partner, but try anyway by first replying to box no. 7637.
Include a full list of qualifications, your aspirations, and a
full frontal nude body shot.

---

21 *The Man From U.N.C.L.E.* – NBC television series broadcast between 1964
and 1968 and centred upon a two-man troubleshooting team working for the
covert organization United Network Command for Law and Enforcement.
The Fresh Prince of Bel-Air – NBC television series running from 1990 to 1996.
The programme was a comedy based around the cultural tensions of a street-
wise teenager from West Philadelphia sent to live with his wealthy relatives
in their Bel Air mansion. The main character, Will, was played by Will Smith.
Smith recorded a version of 'Wild Wild West' for the soundtrack of the 1999
Barry Sonnenfeld feature film of the same name (1999, Overbrook/Interscope/
Columbia). The song featured a performance by rap artist Kool Moe Dee,
who sings the chorus from his 1988 song of the same name, taken from Dee's
album *How Ya Like Me Now* (1987, Jive). The chorus features the lyric 'Wicky
wicky wild, wild west'. The song reached number one in the *Billboard* Hot 100.

When not in my London city office overseeing the day-to-day business of my successful accountancy firm, I can be found leaning inside taxi cabs, spitting wild obscenities and challenging the drivers to fisticuffs. M, 47. We take the direct route home, we don't stop at Belisha beacons and we never – and I mean never – leave the impudence of a box junction unquestioned.[22] Don't expect a tip from box no. 9091.

The toughest decision I ever had to make was choosing between soup and fish in a Brighton café in 1987 (I went for the fish, though later regretted my decision when I discovered the cod had been over-seasoned). Now, however, I'll have to pick one of you delicious women. The selection procedure will involve a four-part interview, along with an aptitude test and multiple-choice questionnaire. Apply now for full details to stupid man, 45. Box no. 6821.

This advert is the only feel-good moment in this edition of the *London Review of Books*. Man, 51. Box no. 7251.

They gave me this personal advert for free because I moaned, whinged and complained like a mo' fo'[23] over my last advert not getting any replies. Who's the winner now B? Me. It's me. I'm the winner and don't you ever forget it. Man, 29. Deprived of affection and most forms of human contact since birth, now just wants a ton of free stuff and to be loved. Box no. 8632.

---

22 Belisha beacons – the flashing orange globes on the top of black and white poles at British and Irish pedestrian traffic-crossing systems, or zebra crossings. They are named after Leslie Hore-Belisha, the Minister of Transport between 1934 and 1937, who introduced them.

23 mo' fo' – abbreviation of the gang expletive 'motherfucker'.

Like the previous advertiser, but +1. Box no. 2850.

If you don't love yourself, I can't love you. Although
I'm still quite happy to have sex. As long as you buy me
dinner. And theatre tickets. And a new pair of trousers.
And a fridge magnet that says 'Sagittarians do it with a
quiver'. Man, 36. Happy to hook up with needy, desperate,
confidence-lacking fems to 40 until someone better comes
along. Box no. 9721.

I wrote this advert specifically to rebuke my rivals,
undermine my critics, and fill the hearts and minds of my
true followers with the love they so richly deserve. Kevin,
46, Sunbury Cross. Box no. 9811.

That darksome cave they enter, where they find / That
cursèd man, low sitting on the ground, / Musing full sadly
in his sullen mind.[24] So, next time you want to turn the TV
over, ask first. Finchley troll (35). Box no. 1117.

Nineties upper-class Poll Tax rebel – 'can pay, but
chooses not to so as to gain working-class affinity.'[25]
Strictly red wine socialists only write to M thirties before
father's publishing company pays him to trek across the
Hindu Kush and write jejune diaries. Box no. 0521.

Once was wonderful. Twice was terrific. But a third?
That's just damned crazy. Serial husband hoping for Home

---

24 Taken from Book I, Canto ix, stanza 35 of Edmund Spenser's *The Faerie
Queene* (see p. 15, n. 1).

25 'Can't pay, won't pay' was the slogan used by protesters during the Poll
Tax (also known as 'Community Charge') protests of 1989 and 1990. The tax
was widely unpopular, seemingly shifting the tax burden from rich to poor,
and is cited as one of the contributing factors in the downfall of the Thatcher
government.

Counties hat-trick.[26] Would-be match-ball wives write to objectionable sexist pig, box no. 0121.

I couldn't care less. This message is paid for by the Apathetic Old Shits Society. Box no. 5102.

Beard. Real ale. A load of bollocks about Marx. Short-lived sexual intercourse. You have to admire my honesty. Now get the drinks in. Man, 43, Camden. Box no. 9219.

Narcissus of Truro.[27] Likes nothing better than admiring himself, but hopes gay man to 45 will rest contented as a close second. Box no. 8336.

26   Hat-trick is the term used to describe a set of three goals by a single player in an association football match. Players who score a hat-trick are entitled to keep the ball used during the game.

27   Truro – administrative centre of the county of Cornwall. It is twinned with Boppard, Rhineland-Palatinate, Germany, and Morlaix, Brittany, France, after which Morlaix Avenue in Truro is named.

"Primal scream therapy among the pots of flat-leaf parsley"

These adverts give birth to a thousand violent dreams.
And when I awake I am no longer immune to the desperate
cries of the damned. After-dinner speaker and corporate
entertainer (M, 57) seeks lover/CV-writer/exorcist for
nights of re-aligning my career path and silencing the
voices. Box no. 8558.

If we hit it off and embark on a serious relationship, I
must insist that you don't throw surprise birthday parties
for me when I've just been turned down for the role of
Leroy in my local church drama group's production of
Fame.[28] Man, 63, harbouring a more lateral standard of
psychological episode triggers. Eccleston. Box no. 8088.

My last chance to leave home died in a house fire in 1978,
along with two cats, a goldfish called Herod, and my VAT
receipts for the previous financial year. Since then I'm not
allowed to leave my mother alone. Or use matches. Or
flammable nylons. I'm also not allowed anywhere near
spoons, but that's another story. You can hear all about it
by replying to mitten-wearing idiot man (51), Gloucester
borders. Box no. 9997.

No obligation whatsoever to marry lonely, desperate
and emotionally draining 42-year-old Oxford academic
and produce children for him in the next couple of years.
Relationship strictly in your own time (but it's a long ride

---

28 *Fame* – US television series running from 1982 to 1987. The show was
based on the 1980 motion picture of the same name (dir. Alan Parker) that tells
the stories of the students and faculty at the New York City High School for the
Performing Arts. The character, Leroy Johnson, was a street-wise performer
who possessed no formal training but had an abundance of raw dancing talent.
He was played in both the series and film by Gene Anthony Ray (1962–2003).

and the meter's running). You've absolutely nothing to
lose (except the respect of your parents and a few of your
friends). Box no. 0413.

Did you just look at that other advert? Don't lie, I saw
you. Paranoid, jealous and often scary woman, 42. Do you
want this marriage to work or not? You don't know the
meaning of love. London – so why does your credit card
receipt say 'Birmingham'? Box no. 1118.

I've spent my adult life fabricating reciprocal feelings
from others and I don't intend to stop now, nor at any
other London Review Bookshop event I'm summarily
ejected from. Yes, once the history section had emptied
and we were left alone his voice said 'I'm not interested',
but his eyes very clearly stated 'please follow me home at a
discreet distance and secretly observe me from the shrubs
in the park opposite.' Woman, 43. Reading between the
lines even when the lines aren't actually there. Don't
pretend you don't love me. Box no. 7966.

If we meet, it mustn't conflict with my community service
obligations. Edgy woman (51), not terribly fond of over-
hanging hedgerows or cats or postmen WLTM man to 55
who has other things to do for ninety hours over the next
three months. Box no. 3039.

I've kissed too many frogs in search of my prince.
Woman, 32. Retired from amphibian zoology very much
against her will. Box no. 3332.

The average person contains enough iron in their body to make a small nail. Not me, I've got about a tent peg's worth. Man, 57, enjoys licking railings.[29] Box no. 3352.

If you think I'm going to love you – you're right. Clingy, over-emotional and socially draining woman, 36. Once you've got me, you can never ever leave me. Not ever. Prone to maniacal bursts of crying, usually followed by excitable and uncontrollable laughter. Life is a rollercoaster; you've just got to ride it, as Ronan Keating once said.[30] Buxton. Box no. 0617.

If you respond to this ad and agree to meet me, you'll probably want to get yourself drunk first. Man, 51. Good-looking but rarely great with conversation. Especially if it doesn't require me thumbing nervously through the Welsh coastal tides timetable that I always carry in my wallet next to a picture of my mother (may the Lord have mercy on her sweet soul, snatched injudiciously away from us by ulcer complications on June 17th, 1987 – we love you, Mum, you're with us every single day). Box no. 9291.

I am not as high maintenance as my highly polished and impeccably arranged collection of porcelain cats suggests, but if you touch them I will kill you. F, 36. Likes porcelain cats. Seeks man not unused to the sound of

---

29 The body contains between 3.5 and 4.5 grams of iron, two-thirds of which is present in haemoglobin. The remainder is stored in the liver, spleen, and bone-marrow. A small amount is present as myoglobin, which acts as an oxygen store in muscle tissue. Four grams of iron would be sufficient to make a small-gauge nail measuring approximately 1.91 centimetres (¾ inch) in length.

30 The advertiser quotes a lyric from 'Life is a Rollercoaster', written by Gregg Alexander and Rick Nowels. Performed by Ronan Keating on his album *Ronan* (2000, Polydor). The single reached number one in the UK singles chart.

sobbing coming from a bedroom from which he is strictly prohibited. Tell me how attractive I am at box no. 1123.

Justify my strop.[31] PMS 24/7 suffering woman seeks man to 35 prone to inadvertently saying the wrong thing (which is everything) at the wrong time (which is always). No whistling. You have been warned. Chocolate (lots of it, please) to box no. 3234.

Let's wipe the slate clean. Lacklustre, melancholic and depressive rock-climbing PhD (M, 29) unable to get a foothold in anything seeks woman with those funny metal things that stab into crevices and stop you from plummeting to a certain death.[32] Or whatever the hell it is they're called. Box no. 7712.

My complex personality permits both inane conversations about meaningful topics and meaningful conversations about inane topics. More unusually, it also harbours a fear of ceramic tiles. Women to 50 – laminate your kitchens then let's spend hours talking about the identity of the fifth Beatle.[33] M, 51, Ross-on-Wye. Box no. 9927.

31 'Justify My Love' – written by Ingrid Chavez, Lenny Kravitz, and Madonna. Taken from the Madonna album *The Immaculate Collection* (1990, Sire, Warner Bros). It reached number one in the *Billboard* Hot 100 and became the highest-selling video single of all time.

32 Camming device invented by Soviet mountaineer and inventor Vitaly Mikhaylovich Abalakov in the 1930s. Abalakov was arrested by the NKVD (People's Commissariat for Internal Affairs) in 1938 along with other members of his team. They remained under investigation until 1940, being accused of 'open public propaganda' of Western mountaineering techniques and 'diminishing' domestic alpinists' achievements, and also of being German spies. Many of the alpinists arrested with Abalakov were executed but he survived the investigation and went on to be awarded the Order of Lenin (1957), Order of the Badge of Honour (1972) and the titles Honoured Master of Sports of the USSR (1943) and Honoured Trainer of the USSR (1961). He died in 1986.

33 After they were inducted into the Rock and Roll Hall of Fame in 1988, the Beatles' George Harrison said that there were only two 'fifth Beatles', Neil

I'm placing this ad against my better judgment. But then the last time I listened to my better judgment it told me the only way to find a well-read articulate man to 45 was to hide in a bin outside his flat until he arrived home from work then lunge wildly at him as he struggled to put the key in his door. If the ad doesn't work, keep your bins inside until collection day. Woman, 43. Tactile and cuddly in a mildly terrifying sort of way. Box no. 8629.

The Owl Who Married a Goose. National Film Board of Canada bore seeks woman who ideally has a shed full of public information films and a ravenous appetite for animated shorts that heavily rely upon waltzes. The modern world has deserted us, leaving us free to create our own Cosmic Zoom.[34] Professional therapists welcome. Box no. 8381.

I sense a lot of sadness behind most of these ads. Not this one though – I'm double-dosed until next spring's repeat prescription review. Happy woman, 34. This dainty, girlish laugh isn't forever, and I'll blame you when it ends,

Aspinall and Derek Taylor, but there have been many (often dubious) claimants to the title. These include, at various stages, Muhammad Ali, Pete Best, Wilfrid Brambell, William Stuart Campbell, Eric Clapton, Rod Davis, Brian Epstein, Mal Evans, Astrid Kirchherr, Len Garry, Eric Griffiths, Colin Hanton, Nicky Hopkins, Tatsuya Ishida, Larry Kane, Jackie Lomax, Jeff Lynne, Linda McCartney, George Martin, Tommy Moore, Murray the K, Chas Newby, Jimmy Nicol, Yoko Ono, Billy Preston (sometimes cited as 'the Black Beatle'), Little Richard, Ed Rudy, Tony Sheridan, Pete Shotton, Phil Spector, Stuart Sutcliffe, James Taylor, Klaus Voormann, Andy White, and Roby Yonge.

34 National Film Board of Canada – public film distribution and production organization operating as an agency of the government of Canada. It is better known for documentaries and animated short films, many of which have gained cult status. Two such examples are cited in the advert – *The Owl Who Married a Goose* (1974, dir. Caroline Leaf), an Inuit legend animated with Inuktitut voices, and *Cosmic Zoom* (1968, dir. Eva Szasz), a short animated feature exploring the magnitude of space and the minuteness of matter.

but by then we'll have a mortgage and a massive debt and you won't ever be able to escape. Box no. 9911.

....

Frau Emmy of Colchester (38) seeks non-talking cure for evenings of nachträglichkeit.[35] Why put off until tomorrow what you can do next week? Box no. 5520.

....

I trew there's charm in a wee pickle gear, / And wha wadna strive at the gaining o't? It mak's a puir body baith canty and fier, / If honesty's had the obtaining o't.[36] You know what I'm saying. Woman, 43. Possibly mad. Livingstone. Box no. 4424.

....

Some incidents in life are blacked-out for a reason. Much as I shudder to recall an incident at Dulwich in 1968 involving a goose, a penny whistle and the local priest, so you will probably twist in the wind whenever, in years to come, you're forced to relate a tale about how you once replied to a personal advert in a flurry of misplaced appreciation for what you regarded at the time as a heightened and sophisticated sense of irony. Man, 40. Hates geese. And priests. And penny whistles. Box no. 7793.

....

35 Frau Emmy was the pseudonym given to Sigmund Freud's patient Fanny Moser, who was presented to Freud exhibiting sequences of facial tics and stammers that today would be diagnosed as a form of Tourette's syndrome. *Nachträglichkeit* is a psychoanalytic conception of time indicating 'deferred action' and used to refer to the relationship between an event and its later meaning in an individual's life. Freud used the term *nachträglichkeit* in many of his published works, but the word is absent in the index of his *Gesammelte Werke*, possibly indicating that he didn't feel the subject had sufficient conceptual substance to warrant a paper on it. Colchester has a population of 104,390.

36 Taken from 'The Best Thing Wi' Gear Is the Haining O't', a traditional Scottish folksong about thriftiness written by Archibald McKay and published in his book *Ingle-Side Lilts* (1855).

This advert is exactly what happens when local councils release man-eating squirrels into the wild to do the jobs that men used to do. Do you hear me, Corrie McChord? Do you? Man, 37. Proudly staring the squirrels in the face and telling them, 'Not today, motherfuckers, not today.' Stirling.[37] Box no. 8822.

I begin each sexual performance with a tympani roll. I find it steadies the ship. Less than buoyant canal-boat dweller, amateur percussionist and bon viveur (M, 57) seeks not-easily intimidated woman to 55 with no small knowledge of crank-shaft engines, blue-note fades and behaviour-correcting medicines. Box no. 6362.

Everyone in this column has an agenda. Not me. Man, 41. Box no. 6900.

This time next week you'll think replying to this advert was the best decision you've ever made. At the same time you'll be regretting your choice of footwear. Why? Because dark soles aren't allowed on my mother's newly laid laminates. Don't worry, I've already bought you slippers (size four) and pyjamas (size ten) and a brush for your beautiful long red hair (I've had 'Susan' engraved on the handle – that's what I'd like to call you). Size ten Susans with size four feet, please, reply to box no. 9396. You can be any age but if you're 42 with a birthday on September 6 it will be a distinct advantage. Otherwise we can just pretend.

Love? My eyes will tell you all. My forehead, however, is slightly more reticent. My knees won't give you a damn

---

37   Corrie McChord – leader of Stirling Council in Scotland. Squirrels are omnivorous.

word. Paranoid military nutcase and part-time undertaker seeks F to 50. Box no. 2122.

....

Tomatoes of wrath. Angry organic window-box farmer (M, 51, Hersham). Seeking green-fingered, red-eyed, purple-standing-out-on-forehead-veined woman for evenings of primal scream therapy among the pots of flat-leaf parsley. Must have own trowel. Box no. 0915.

"Scrimshawed from the tusk of a walrus"

This advert originally contained a 300-word paragraph about cats but I edited it out. Woman, 36. Box no. 5637.

I stopped playing Freecell[38] for three-and-a-quarter hours to write this ad. Man, 39. Box no. 9763.

This ad is emblematic of, yet somehow transcends, my entire body of work. Magician and part-time shrimp peeler (M, 48). Tring. Box no. 8522.

This advert was constructed specifically to attract the exactly right sort of person by utilising the very subtle tenets of Feng Shui.[39] Woman, 52. Box no. 0778.

I scrimshawed this advert from the tusk of a walrus. Now make love to me. Pathetic man, 49. Box no. 6758.

This advert first appeared in this column in 2001. I've rehashed and updated it, however, replacing the original cast with a man who is now 37 rather than 32. And he's seeking any form of female contact rather than just a rich, 21-year old blonde woman able to apply Pilates techniques to intimate moments.[40] Oh, and his waist is now four

---

38 Solitaire-based card game included on Windows computer packages. The original version consisted of 32,000 possible combinations of play, of which only game #11,982 was unbeaten. Later editions carried approximately 1,000,000 combinations, where games #11,982, #146,692, #186,216, #455,889, #495,505, #512,118, #517,776 and #781,948 are thought to be unsolvable.

39 Feng Shui – ancient Chinese system of aesthetics used to harmonize the flow of life-energy (or chi) in a living or working environment.

40 Physical fitness regime that focuses on the core postural muscles. It was developed by Joseph Pilates during the First World War to help rehabilitate returning veterans.

inches wider. And he's defaulted on most of his credit cards. Box no. 6201.

. . . .

I stole the contents of this ad from a highly successful banker (M, 53, annual income £500k + benefits) currently appearing on Match.com.[41] It's funny because we honestly couldn't be more different. Unless I was a woman. Or 12. Man. Older than 12 and not really a banker. Box no. 3469.

. . . .

My psychotherapist suggested I place this ad. Woman, 43. Not mental, despite whatever a fear of open spaces, the colour red, the sound of rain, plastic containers, beards, percussionists, birdsong and cornflakes may suggest. Box no. 4326.

. . . .

This advert began as a limp but over the following weeks it developed into this magnificent sprint. Woman, 36. Probably as good as you'll ever get. Stop complaining and kiss me. Box no. 0880.

. . . .

I had to take part-time work to pay for this advert. F, 32. Box no. 7710.

. . . .

I spent an entire day in the British Library sourcing obscure reference material to cite in this ad, then I lost it all when I stopped off at Burger King on the way home. Man, 34. Box no. 8611.

. . . .

I wrote this ad to prove I'm not gay. Man, 29. Not gay. Absolutely not. Box no. 7471.

. . . .

I grazed my knee writing this advert. Accident prone F, 35. Box no. 4311.

. . . .

41   Match.com – online dating service begun in 1994.

In laboratory tests, this ad made seven mice blind. The remaining three, however, developed extra-sensory powers and the ability to levitate. You could too, by replying to excommunicated biologist and psychic-mouse groomer (M, 39) at box no. 4656. Or you may just go blind. It's a 70–30 shot but you can't halt progress.

**"Sexually,
I'm more of a
Switzerland"**

My subscription to the LRB includes a proviso allowing time for 'quiet naps'. That pretty much says everything you need to know. Man. Box no. 7429.

My self-compiled love-making tape includes songs from the lesser known albums of Crosby, Stills and Nash.[42] Man, 48. Box no. 8595.

They don't call me Naughty Lola. They call me Brian. Brian, 57.[43] Box no. 6477.

Correct me if I'm wrong, but I think this personal advert puts me firmly on the map. Box no. 8541.

Are you more Peret than du Pré? More mocha than Moët? More Bacardi Breezer than Bollinger? Then write to me, F, 46, more Judith Chalmers than Judith Pinnow.[44] Box no. 3733.

England's best hope for Olympic gold if ever there was an Olympic event for wearing plaid and brogues. Man, 56. Not a snappy dresser but extremely well-endowed. Box no. 9987.

The wind left my sails years ago. Hopeless yachtsman (M, 64). Box no. 8521.

42 The advertiser is possibly referring to some of the less commercially successful albums of Crosby, Stills & Nash, namely *After the Storm* (1994), which reached number 98 in the US album charts, and *Live It Up* (1990), which reached number 57.

43 See p. 25, n. 15.

44 Judith Chalmers (b. 1936) – television presenter. Judith Pinnow (b. 1973) – German actress and author.

Think of every sexual partner you've ever had. I'm nothing like them. Unless you've ever slept with a bulimic German cellist called Elsa. Elsa: bulimic German cellist, (F, 37). Box no. 6327.

Did you march in the streets in 1968? I did, but with the Barrow-in-Furness Majorettes. The long white socks and pony-tails have gone, but I can still twirl a baton. If you know how to shine brass buttons, and how to keep a pom-pom fluffy, drop me a line. Box no. 9792.

'Shame' and 'terror'. The two words that most adequately sum up my sexual performances. If yours are 'banter' and 'pot-roast', write now to bubbly F, 36, making trouser-suits from carpet remnants since 1994. Box no. 2525.

Nothing makes me feel more alive than the scent of a well-oiled caster or fake blood spilled clumsily on parkland. Office chair manufacturer and weekend historical battle re-enactor (M, 52) WLTM woman to 50 to join me at Val-ès-Dunes this autumn and witness Duke William the Bastard crush the Norman rebels before we whiz around tiled surfaces on a new pair of reclining lock orthopaedic support seats. No time-wasters.[45] Box no. 8422.

It's a jungle out there! Confused librarian. F, 34. Box no. 7421.

---

45 William the Bastard – latterly King William I, also known as William the Conqueror. With the assistance of King Henry I of France, William secured control of Normandy by defeating rebel Norman barons at Caen in the Battle of Val-ès-Dunes in 1047, obtaining the Truce of God, which was backed by the Roman Catholic Church. The battle is depicted on the Bayeux Tapestry. At the time of the battle, William was Duke of Normandy, having succeeded to the title as the illegitimate son of the previous Duke, Robert I, in 1035.

The song that most puts me in the mood for love is Rick Dees' *Disco Duck*.[46] Woman, 54, clinging desperately to the erotic undertones of a 1976 historical society Christmas party chance dance floor encounter. Box no. 5222.

If I were a hamburger, I'd probably come without the salad stuff. If you like hamburgers without the salad stuff, why not write? Woman, 35. The poorest opening gambits you ever did hear. Box no. 8550.

Yes, the jacket's tweed, the pullover maroon, and the socks over-washed red. But my vest is 100 per cent cotton-twist, and my pants are Primark classics.[47] M, 38. As enticing as a philosophy lecturer can be. Box no. 2116.

Casanova began his career as a librarian.[48] I've begun mine as a museum curator, which is more or less the same thing except it involves old bones and stuff instead of books. And there is a designated picnic area in a museum whereas libraries don't like you bringing in food. And we have fun maps you can colour in as you go around. And help points for the disabled. Man, 24. Museum curator and potential Casanova. Box no. 7971.

---

46 'Disco Duck' – written and performed by Rick Dees and performed by Rick Dees & His Cast of Idiots (1976, Fretone, later RSO). Rigdon Osmond 'Rick' Dees III was a radio DJ at WMPS-AM in Memphis, Tennessee. The song reached number one in the *Billboard* charts in the US in October that year and can be heard in a brief scene in the film *Saturday Night Fever* in which a small group of older people are learning to 'move their feet to the disco beat'.

47 Primark – budget clothing retailer trading in the UK and Ireland (where it is known as Penney's).

48 Giacomo Girolamo Casanova (1725–98). Casanova became a librarian to Count Joseph Karl von Waldstein in the Castle of Dux, Bohemia, in 1785 after many aborted careers, including those of scribe, military officer, violinist and professional gambler.

In France, it's just a kiss. In England it's just a muffin. In Belgium it's just a waffle. In Germany it's just a shepherd. You know what I'm saying. Man, 41. Box no. 5520.

Sexually, I'm more of a Switzerland. F, 54. Box no. 8828.

Does sex have to rear its ugly head? Physically distant, cold, unendearing woman (my age is my business), WLTM man who knows where the door is and when to use it. Sshh – I'm trying to read, and I have to be up early in the morning. Box no. 1009.

Marcel Mauss-type figure (man, 52). Nothing up my sleeve save a love of atonal jazz and a passion for Cup-a-Soup.[49] WLTM woman with knowledge of microwaveable foods and tapered decks. Box no. 9971.

Colour-blind driving instructor and weekend hastilude enthusiast (M, 33) seeks jousting F to 35 to give him the green light (and appropriate 'drive on' hand signal). Box no. 9643.

Although this is an advert that screams excitement, the man who placed it (historian, 54, enjoys model airplanes) is strangely subdued. Box no. 7735.

Man, 46. Animal in bed. Probably a gnu. Box no. 1910.

Serial winner of Alan Bennett audio books in work's Christmas tombola.[50] WLTM man willing to exchange his

---

49 Marcel Mauss (1872–1950) – French sociologist not known for his skills in magic. Cup-a-Soup – instant soup product not known for its microwaveability.

50 Alan Bennett (b. 1934) – author, actor, and playwright.

decade's worth of Marks & Spencer bath bombs, then love the dowager's hump right off of me. Box no. 1014.

Amyl nitrite. Apparently it's not a common rose-fertilizing compound. Write now to box no. 3012 for more ill-judged assumptions made by F, 48, spending weekends going through her ex-husband's 'gardening' drawer. Ben Wa is not a modern-day Percy Thrower.[51]

When the switch is in the 'T' position the microphone is disconnected and no sound is heard from the aid because the microphone has been replaced by a pick-up coil. My explanation for 13 years of pweeeeeph sounds coming from my head during periods of sexual excitement. Now Bluetooth enabled and finally ready to love again. Man, 63, wrestling with the wonders of the modern world like a naked Amazonian might wrestle with angry snakes. Box no. 1211.

---

51 Amyl nitrite – a potent vasodilator often used as a recreational sex drug; known sometimes as poppers. Inhaled, it expands the blood vessels and lowers blood pressure, resulting in the relaxation of involuntary muscles, particularly in the anal sphincter. Ben Wa balls – small metal or plastic balls, usually hollow and containing a small weight that rolls around. Used for sexual stimulation by insertion into the vagina or anus. Percy Thrower MBE (1913–88) – gardener and broadcaster. He was the resident gardener on BBC Television's children's programme *Blue Peter* between 1974 and 1987.

"One eye on the William Hill Saturday quick-pick cards"

Worse things could happen. You could lose all your money on a holiday fling that sure felt like a good idea at the time – until you try to use your credit cards at the resort. Once-bitten, probably get bitten again intellectual numbskull (M, 36). This time my wallet stays in my pocket. Box no. 7108.

My most humbling moment was the birth of my first grandchild. No! Wait! It was when I won the office Grand National sweepstake in 1999. God bless you, Bobbyjo! Idiot gamer (M, 61). One eye on a meaningful relationship, the other on the William Hill Saturday quick-pick cards.[52] Box no. 5244.

Found love yet? Console yourself with our fabulous range of fitted wardrobes – bookcases made to order, leather-bound executive chairs. Write for free catalogue to desperate salesman, 44, divorced, no access to the kids, sleeping in his mother's Astra. Box no. 0527.

Fidelity. The recognition of the supreme importance of love. Intelligence. Beauty. Sense of humour. Sincerity. An appreciation of good food. A serious interest in some art, trade or hobby. An old-fashioned and wholehearted acceptance of monogamy. Courage.[53] Borderline obsession

---

52 Grand National – a handicap chase run over a distance of four miles four furlongs at Aintree race course in Liverpool every year. It is the most valuable National Hunt horse race in the world. Bobbyjo (ridden by Paul Carberry and trained by Tommy Carberry) was the winner in 1999 at race-time odds of 15–1. William Hill PLC is one of the largest chains of bookmakers in the UK.

53 Rudolph Valentino's ten attributes of the perfect woman, cited in *Vanity Fair: Selections from America's Most Memorable Magazine: A Cavalcade of the 1920s and 1930s*, ed. Cleveland Amory and Frederic Bradlee (Viking Press, New York, 1960).

with receipt collecting and completely unfounded fear of calculators. Formerly Rudolph Valentino-type M (32), latterly tax evading, nervous asthmatic (47). Seeks woman not unused to hiding under the kitchen table when the doorbell rings. Box no. 2211.

I am Mr Right! You are Miss Distinct Possibility. Your parents are Mr and Mrs Obscenely Rich. Your uncle is Mr Expert Tax Lawyer. Your cousin is Ms Spare Apartment On A Caribbean Hideaway That She Rarely Uses. Your brother is Mr Can Fix You Up A Fake Passport For A Small Fee. Man, 51. Box no. 1407.

Let's double down on Fifth Street, split the aces on a quad and steal the brag from Napoleon before he freezes out on fourth. Rubbish poker player (M, 41) WLTM women to 45 who aren't too embarrassed to play Connect Four.[54] Box no. 7961.

Fame? Riches? Glamour and a lifetime of ease and comfort? I'd give it all up just to be near you. Freeloading

---

54 Double down – term used in the game blackjack, where the wager is increased to a maximum of double the original bet and the player increasing the wager takes just one more card. Fifth Street – the final single community card played in Texas hold 'em poker games, also called the 'river'. Split aces – in blackjack a player may split their hand if they have been dealt two cards of the same value, giving the opportunity to play two hands. Experts usually recommend splitting aces and eights. Quads – four cards of the same value (in poker). Steal the brag – call someone's bluff. Napoleon – Napoléon Bonaparte (1769–1821), French military and political leader. Freeze out – a game where players start with specific amounts of chips and can buy no more. Fourth – Fourth Street, first board card after the flop in hold 'em, also known as the 'turn'. Connect Four – two-player game in which the players take turns in dropping alternating coloured discs (commonly red and yellow) into a seven-column, six-row vertically-suspended grid. The object of the game is to be the first player to connect four singly-coloured discs in a row. The game was published under the Connect Four trademark by Milton Bradley in 1974; the original version is known as 'The Captain's Mistress'.

loller (38) seeks big breasted celebrity heiress of unfeasibly large fortune (21, max, or I'm out of here). Box no. 5285.

The eighties never went away! Nor did its hair! Or its piano-key tie! Its previously untarnished track record of solvency did though. As did its trousers. And teeth. Man, 47. Less A Flock of Seagulls, more A Troubling of Goldfinches.[55] Box no. 9620.

I hate you, Ray Romano. Woman, 32. One-time publishing high-flier, now redundant and spending most days shouting at the TV. Would like to meet anyone with a decent array of credit cards and no prior experience of the hypnotic ways of QVC.[56] Box no. 0981.

According to my records your Council Tax instalments have not been paid in accordance with the details shown on your bill. Payment of the amount now due must be made within 7 days. Legal proceedings will be commenced 14 days after the date of issue of this notice. If the Council issues a summons, application will be made to the Court for an order for costs from you. Not even love can come between me and my work, but promise you'll try. Responses should be directed to North London council worker (F, 37), box no. 0305. A delay in your response will result in you losing your right to pay future demands by instalments.[57]

55 A Flock of Seagulls – 1980s New Wave band from Liverpool.

56 Ray Romano (b. 1957) – American actor and stand-up comedian best known for his role as the lead character in the CBS sitcom *Everybody Loves Raymond*. QVC – home-shopping channel founded by Joseph Segel in 1986 and broadcast in the US, the UK, Germany, and Japan to a combined audience of 141 million. QVC is an acronym for 'Quality, Value, Choice'.

57 Council Tax – system of local taxation used in England, Scotland, and Wales. It came into effect in 1992, replacing the Community Charge (see p. 33, n. 25). The advertiser is quoting from a Council Tax late-payment notice.

Come fly with me.[58] Man, 42, seeks undemanding tax exile in exotic far-away land (i.e., not the Isle of Man). No money in the bank, but Air Miles-a-go-go at box no. 1008.

The finest mind in the academic world conceived this ad, but it was his secretary who took two and half hours out of her day to collate his angst-ridden ramblings, phone the LRB and pay for it with her own money. He's basically looking for an affair with a twenty-something idiot tart who needs good grades. I'm looking for a better job, a decent pension package, and a man to 50 who's great in bed and doesn't make condescending comments about every damn book I read. Man, 57. Or his secretary, 43. Box no. 1207.

Play your cards right and I'll marry you. Compulsive gambling F, 41, seeks non-judgmental M to whatever with fully functional credit cards, easily remembered pin number, and desperately poor tolerance of alcohol. Also seeking lateral thinking lawyer with track record of successful implausible embezzlement defence claims. Box no. 9876.

Does that billet doux you're writing have my box number on it (M, 42, great eyes, great prospects)? Are you sending it today? Can you enclose a £10 postal order with it – I'm a bit strapped until giro day?[59] Box no. 1208.

---

58 'Come Fly with Me' – composed by Jimmy Van Heusen with lyrics by Sammy Cahn. Performed by Frank Sinatra on his album *Come Fly with Me* (1958, Capitol).

59 Giro day – recipients of unemployment benefit (Jobseeker's Allowance, colloquially known as the 'dole') were paid their fortnightly benefit by giro cheque. Thus the day when a claimant's state benefit is received is sometimes known as 'giro day'. This is still often the case even though electronic transfers

Rich old buggers about to peg it, write to attractive, nubile young filly. Box no. 0119.

Social parasite (M, 36, lecturer in Classics), takes more from the community than he could ever put back. Enjoy it while it's free, I say. WLTM woman compelled to give, give, give. London, or else you pick me up and bring me back. In your own car. Using your own petrol money. Box no. 0916.

What a difference a junior suite makes! That's where you come in – F to 30 with access to husband's bank account and a shrill delight at the thought of breaking through its previously unbreakable overdraft limit over the course of a weekend fling with limber octogenarian bankrupt no longer welcome in his son-in-law's Lake District caravan. Box no. 4328.

Read the small-print before writing any cheques! Bankrupted timeshare-buying moron (41) would like to meet wealthy, blind, deaf, idiotic 96-year-old woman with heart problems. Must be willing to run 20 miles a day and carry the shopping home. Box no. 0919.

And the award for Reformed Criminal Mastermind goes to box no. 0415. (Send signed blank cheques as congratulations.)

In *Analects*, Confucius wrote 'Man has three ways of acting wisely. First, on meditation; that is the noblest. Secondly, on imitation; that is the easiest. Thirdly, on experience; that is the bitterest'.[60] I'd like to add a fourth, on my

---

have, by and large, replaced much of the giro payment system to benefit claimants.

60 Written over a period of thirty to fifty years during the Warring States Period (ca. 479 BC to ca. 221 BC), the *Analects* is the representative work of

patent-pending Decision Squid. Simply place the decision squid in a large water tank with each side labelled with one of the following: 'Yes', 'No', 'Maybe' and 'Decision Squid too tired to answer'. Next, jab the squid with the Question Stick and whichever side it swims to gives you your decision. Man, 36. Bankrupt and recovering alcoholic. Box no. 8785.

LRB subscribers – get six free issues and your money back if you're not entirely satisfied with Market Rasen[61] lust racoon (M, 78) – 'The most serious and radical lust racoon around'. Direct debit forms, and dried fruit, to box no. 8620.

Publishing's Next Big Thing (October, 1998). One time author and bon viveur (M, 37) now part-time baguette filler and amateur chiropractor seeks agent who actually will call Monday[62]/career advisor/solvent woman with impressive stock options and low self-esteem. Box no. 9997.

Confucianism. The Chinese title literally means 'discussion over Confucius' words'.

61   Market Rasen is a town and civil parish within the West Lindsey district of Lincolnshire. It lies on the River Rase 13.8 miles (22 km) northeast of Lincoln, 18 miles (29 km) east of Gainsborough and 16.3 miles (26 km) southwest of Grimsby. Its population is 3,200.

62   Possibly a reference to one of the world's largest talent and literary agencies, International Creative Management. ICM is sometimes referred to by its clients as 'I'll Call Monday'.

"Only love is catching"

There aren't enough hours in the day for me to make love to all the women I want to make love to, so I'm going to start with you, nubile 21-year-old choreographer and tantric masseuse, preferably French or able to adopt a French accent or not talk at all. Must know how to spoon-feed. Man, 78. Box no. 4876.

Like a lot of people, I'm uncomfortable in my own skin. Unlike a lot of people it's because I have an unidentified skin allergy that has baffled science for 47 years. Woman, 47. Itchy and baffling. Box no. 8369.

I took steroids to produce this winner of an ad. Woman, 64. Box no. 4976.

Shepherd of Love seeks F to 45 free of scrapie, pinkeye and Caseous Lymphadenitis.[63] Vet (M, 43). Little experience of human contact outside the farming communities of Pembs. Box no. 9837.

Walk a mile in another man's shoes. Mine. But only if I can borrow your trousers. And a cummerbund if you have one. Syndicated clothing enthusiast and mature student radiologist on the verge of finally graduating to the big leagues (Haversham General Hospital) WLTM woman with 42-inch waist and 30-inch inside leg, or man with size

---

63 Scrapie – a fatal, degenerative disease that affects the nervous systems of sheep and goats. Pinkeye – a highly contagious infection of sheep and goats and humans that affects the eye and surrounding structures. Caseous lymphadenitis (CLA) – a disease caused by the bacterium *Corynebacterium pseudotuberculosis*. It commonly leads to the formation of abscesses within the lymph nodes and lungs and sometimes other organs of sheep and goats.

six brogues, or anyone with an over-active thyroid and a plaid jacket in XL. No loons. Box no. 8974.

Not all that wheezes is asthma. Laryngologist and weekend chicken-farmer (M, 61) seeks attractive F to 70 with stable blood pressure for long distance running, evening tango classes and CPR. Box no. 8369.

Michelle Barrow of Class 4C: yes, astigmatism is permanent, but so is chess-genius. Unlike sports ability or hair. Who's laughing now? Not Jamie MacFarlane of Windsor Keys-While-U-Wait, that's for sure. Box no. 7863.

You'll have to speak louder than that to be heard above my tinnitus. Tinnitus-suffering woman, 40. Box no. 8631.

X-rays, blood tests, EEGs, ECGs, lung function, barium, bone density, colonoscopy. Doctors don't know what to do with me. Medical enigma (M, 33). Confounding science and all the staff at Streatham Hill Burger King since 1997. Box no. 9731.

Does anyone know what I did last summer?[64] Kitsch horror-fan and recovering alcoholic (M, 52). Box no. 9722.

Last time I placed an advert in here I got a great response from a lovely man who seemed ideal (remember those letters, swapping bits of Yeats with lines from Dylan songs?). We arranged to meet at a nice restaurant south of the Thames. Unfortunately I missed the date because on

---

64   Reference to the 1997 horror film *I Know What You Did Last Summer* (dir. Jim Gillespie).

the way out of my flat I popped a Kegel.[65] That was almost three years ago, but after several surgical pubococcygeus restorative procedures and 30 months of contracting and relaxing and stopping mid-flow I'm finally ready for that Italian meal you promised. If you're still out there, Carl from Highbury, get in touch with Wendy, now 49 and fit enough downstairs to crack a walnut. Otherwise any man to 55 who isn't afraid of surgical knickers. Box no. 9376.

I could fit into a 42-inch-waist trouser if I sucked in a little. Pathetic man, mid-eighties (GI value of typical breakfast), mid-fifties (temperature after walking upstairs), 143 (heart rate after walking upstairs), 38 (minutes before coming around after walking upstairs, and my age). WLTM patient F in a bungalow. Box no. 0295.

I got it bad and that ain't good.[66] Amateur jazz singer (F, 54) seeks glockenspielist/gynaecologist for nights of atonal ramblings through both my medicine cabinet and your prescription pad. No crazies. Box no. 8632.

One day this advert will have its own entry on Wikipedia for gaining the most responses ever received. Reply now to get to the head of the queue. Hay fever-suffering gymnast (M, 52). Box no. 3960.

65   The muscles of the pelvic floor, sometimes known as 'Kegel muscles' after Dr Arnold Kegel, who devised a system of exercises to strengthen weakened pubococcygeus muscles of the pelvic floor.

66   'I Got It Bad (and That Ain't Good)' – jazz standard by Duke Ellington and Paul Francis Webster. Written for Herb Jeffries's *Jump for Joy* revue, which opened on 10 July 1941. The song was originally sung by Ivie Anderson but many notable versions have been recorded since, including that of Nina Simone, which was included on the soundtrack to the Coen brothers' film *The Big Lebowski* (1998).

A list of what I'm looking for in a man is displayed on the door of my fridge. You'll never see it, however, because I locked myself out of my flat at the weekend and will probably have to rent somewhere else for a while. Menopausal woman, 52. Sent my Estraderm off to Truprint[67] back in January and now spend most evenings staring in despair at seven rolls of unprocessed Christmas film with no hormonal benefits whatsoever. Box no. 9361.

They said the best way to a man's heart is through his stomach. Disqualified surgeon (F, 32), a touch on the literal side maybe, seeks man for nights of complete misunderstanding. Box no. 0219.

Frankly, I don't think there's anywhere near enough salt in ready meals these days.[68] Man, 37, poor kidney function. Box no. 3976.

What do you get when you fall in love? Trench foot.[69]

67 Estraderm – oestradiol-based sex-hormone medication used as hormone replacement therapy (HRT) in menopausal women. Truprint – mail order and online photograph processing service.

68 The Scientific Advisory Committee on Nutrition (SACN) recommends no more than 4 grams of salt per day (1.6 grams sodium). The Food Safety Authority of Ireland endorses this recommendation. Australia defines a recommended dietary intake (RDI) of 0.92–2.3 grams sodium per day (between 2.3 and 5.8 grams salt). In the United States, the Food and Drug Administration does not make a recommendation but refers readers to Dietary Guidelines for Americans 2005. These suggest that US citizens should consume less than 2.3 grams of sodium (or 5.8 grams salt) per day.

69 'What do you get when you fall in love?' – a line taken from the song 'I'll Never Fall in Love Again', written by Burt Bacharach and Hal David for the musical *Promises, Promises* (1968), based on the Billy Wilder film *The Apartment*. It has been covered by many notable artists, including Bobbie Gentry, who recorded it for her album *Touch 'Em with Love* (1969, EMI). It reached number one in the UK charts. Trench foot – also known as immersion foot. Caused by prolonged exposure of the feet to damp, unsanitary, and cold conditions above freezing point. If left untreated trench foot usually results in gangrene, which

Woman, 36, seeks man to 40 who has no interest in
re-enacting WWI battles and doesn't insist on making love
in sewage-filled holes dug in the garden. Box no. 9271.

The rumours are true! A scintillating love monkey
does read the *London Review of Books* and currently has an
opening in his life for a delicious lust vixen with whom to
super-charge the static on his real nylon sheets. This advert
is the recruitment process and, guess what, you just got the
job (home-owning women or convincing TSs only, 20–65,
verifiable income, full credit history, no pets, no smokers,
some knowledge of pulmonary medical procedures a
distinct advantage). Man, 68. By reading the advert this far
you agree to its terms and conditions and acknowledge it
to be a legally binding contract. No loons. Box no. 8611.

**This advert may well be the Cadillac of all lonely hearts
adverts,** but its driver is the arthritic granddad with a
catalogue of driving convictions. Arthritic granddad
(67) with a catalogue of driving convictions including
'Driving whilst trying to turn the dang wipers off', 'Driving
whilst wondering if his urology appointment has come
through', and 'Driving whilst "Hey! Isn't that where your
Aunt Maude's first husband lived after the divorce came
through? He's settled in Jersey now. I could never stand
him – he used to do this thing with his teeth . . ." ' WLTM
someone who knows how stop the oven from beeping. Box
no. 9729.

They said I'd never dance again – they were right.
Incontinent 76-year-old man, needs buxom woman to
spoon-feed him breakfast (and dress his leg ulcers). OK,

can require amputation. It was a particular problem for soldiers in trench
warfare during the winters of World Wars I and II and in the Vietnam War.

I'm not Cary Grant, but who are you – Lana Turner? Box no. 0123.

....

Love me, love my fungal skin complaint. Man, 37, charmless and flaky. Box no. 0914.

....

Girlfriend in a coma,[70] mother undergoing angioplasty, father with a bad case of shingles, but there's nothing wrong with me (other than a lazy eye and hay fever). Only love is catching at box no. 1214.

....

70 'Girlfriend in a Coma' – written by Johnny Marr and Morrissey. Performed by The Smiths and taken from their album *Strangeways, Here We Come* (1987, Rough Trade Records). It reached number thirteen in the UK singles chart and became the inspiration for the Douglas Coupland novel of the same name (1998, HarperCollins Canada).

"Look sideways with schadenfreude"

Ten things you should know about me. Favourite read –
Querelle de Brest, Jean Genet. Favourite attribute – my eyes
(hazel). Brand of cigarette – Malboro (red). Phobia –
peristerophobia (look it up). Favourite walk – Lochinver to
Suilven. Favourite food – M&M's (green ones). Favourite
country to visit – Denmark. Allergy – men who earn less
than £80k per annum. I am a woman. I am 37. I can do
a weird trick with my nostrils, a ball of string and seven
paper clips. Now you.[71] Box no. 7626.

Ever woken up and wondered why you have that sinking
feeling again? Ever stopped to think why everything seems
so cold? Ever longed for the warmth of another? Ever just
wanted to be able to give love and to receive a little love
back? Ever married a homosexual? Well I have, buster, so
save the sob-stories. Woman, 52, WLTM man to 60 willing
to participate in an intense program of psychometric
testing including, but not limited to, a polygraph and
a lengthy discussion over wallpaper samples before we
commit to any sort of relationship. Box no. 1109.

Peel half a mango and slice into a blender. Add half a
banana and some slices of apple. Add the juice of half

---

71 In Genet's novel, Querelle is a thief, a prostitute, an opium smuggler and
a serial killer. Ostensibly he kills for money, but his real motive for murder is
pleasure. Peristerophobia – a fear of pigeons. Lochinver (or Loch an Inbhir
in Gaelic) is a village on the coast of Sutherland, Scotland. Green M&M
candies have often been attributed with aphrodisiac qualities. Rumours of
an aphrodisiac association with the green candies began in the 1970s when
students reportedly collected them from packets to feed to their loved ones
during sex. Mars eventually exploited the myth from 1997, when it first
introduced the green character candy into advertising campaigns. By 2001, the
campaigns were much more suggestive. The green M&M character became a
clearly sexualized version of the other characters, with fuller lips, heavy-lidded
eyes, and long eyelashes. The campaign carried the tag-line 'Is it true what they
say about the green ones?'

an orange and a little ginger. Blend with ice. Smoke 17
cigarettes. Drink a bottle of gin. Cry. Phone your mother
and slur incoherently down the receiver. Clean the
aquarium. Steal the neighbour's bin. Get thrown out of
local grocery store. Sleep under some leaves. If your days
begin with the best intentions but gradually unravel, why
not get yourself some psychological help from a trained
professional, rather than from gorgeous, articulate F,
36, with four languages, own home, own business and a
Dutch cap. Box no. 8807.

One night stands based on lust, greed, and mutual
disgust have led to some of the most fulfilling three-hour
sections of my life, but now I'd like a man who knows
how to read and will, eventually, come to learn the entire
layout of my house. That's where you come in, LRB-
reading men to 50 with good incomes, good careers, no
pets and a penchant for women who know exactly the right
tone of whining to get the things they want in life. Box no.
5375.

I've memorised every shortcut to Waitrose, Caversham.[72]
Woman, 43, just about ready to take a step up the social
ladder with any reasonably-minded moneyed M to 90. An
ability to know when not to speak is a distinct advantage,
as are frequent-flyer Air Miles. Box no. 7511.

Whilst calming down after a heated argument involving
smashed plates, thrown cutlery and insults directed at your
circus side-show of a family, you should know now that
I'm very unlikely to participate in that 'no, really, I'm sorry,
it was my fault' charade. You accept all of the blame all of
the time or you grow gills to breathe in the stale, bitter

72 The Caversham branch of Waitrose is located at 51 Church Street.

soup of my angry and eternal silence. Cuddly F, 36, brown hair, green eyes, degree in geology. Box no. 2129.

When we eventually meet for dinner under the pretext of wanting to know each other better before we engage in the self-destructive sex we've each been craving since our previous relationships crashed against the rocks of reality (in my case, a younger, more attractive woman – in your case a stunning lack of awareness that you're not actually the most interesting person in the world), the widening of my eyes and the nodding of my head may be mistaken for me empathizing with whatever banal and ridiculous episode of self-pity you've just launched yourself into. I'm not. I recently started wearing contact lenses to combat the 'anal librarian' features my delightfully eloquent ex-husband so often accused me of having; they irritate my corneas. And that's no smile – it's me trying to pluck a fish rib from my teeth with my tongue. Woman, 39. No time for small-talk at box no. 6637.

Don't look back in anger,[73] try condescension instead. Look sideways with schadenfreude and downward in revulsion. Serial divorcee (F, 53) has you in her sights next with a raft of sarcastic barbs and derisive statements, but a photo sent to box no. 8288 along with a list of trite achievements that I'll remain aloof and casually disdainful about should make the whole process slightly less painful by confronting the inevitable head on.

I beg to differ. Box no. 0535.

---

73 'Don't Look Back in Anger' – written by Noel Gallagher and performed by Oasis. The song appeared on their second album, *(What's the Story) Morning Glory?* (1995, Creation/Big Brother). It reached number one in the UK singles chart.

Woman, 35. Happily married until husband sponsored an African village goat in her name as a birthday gift. WLTM man to 40 for whom the phrase 'I'd really like a pair of diamond earrings' isn't meant ironically. Box no. 7333.

Spend your days looking for an alibi? She's here – 35, dark-haired and smoking twenty a day. It won't save you on divorce lawyers, but it'll stop you shoplifting. Box no. 8122.

Lonely? A yearning heart? Passion wasting away? Tell it to someone who gives a damn. Out there/over here US academic woman, unsentimental but strong like an ox. Can break hearts as well as snap chicken necks. WLTM weak, inconsolable man who knows when he's beat (that's you, fella). Box no. 0316.

Rejection is always the hardest part of a relationship. So unless you're male, 35–40, well-built, intelligent but not intellectually trussed-up like some unendearing Oxbridge bow-tied moneyed ponce who spent their formative years tossing about in Tuscany with an over-flowing allowance from your over-bearing parents who hated you so much they sent you to boarding school, which is where you learned to be ingratiatingly annoying and talk with a disgusting nasal drawl, save yourself the heartache and don't write to happy woman, 35, at box no. 1117.

Democracy doesn't work in a genuinely loving relationship. It creates emotional cholesterol – blocking the arteries of passion with compromise and a fear of upsetting your significant other. So when you eventually complain about me whining, stamping my feet and insisting on getting my own way, really I'm just projecting my love for you and trying to protect the precious thing we have together. Woman, 46. We do things my way, or we don't do them at all. I'm only thinking of us. Yorks. Box no. 4546.

I walk the line between indifference and, meh, whatever. If you're going to write do it quickly. *The OC* is on in half an hour.[74] Woman. Thirties. Box no. 5710.

Most partners cite the importance of having a loved one who will listen and understand them. I'm here to rubbish this theory. The more you listen to your loved one, the more you will realise they talk crap, whine a lot, and make a lot of unreasonable demands regarding holidays together (since when is a car-ferry better than a plane, since when is a museum tour stop better than drunken evenings talking to oiled-up Italians on a beach?). I'd like to state here and now that anyone responding to this advert and winding up in an emotional (or, even better, purely sexual and frequently tawdry) relationship with me will never be listened to at all. That way we can carry on the pretence of enjoying each other's company for many an ignorant year. No lawyers. Woman, 38. Box no. 5002.

Ball-breaking irrational F (52). Very probably just like your mother. Box no. 7911.

I'm everything you ever wanted in a woman. Assuming you're into fat 47-year-old moody bitches who really don't enjoy the mornings. Stop talking and pour the bloody marys at box no. 1908.

---

74 Teen drama that originally aired on the Fox network in the US for four seasons between 2003 and 2007.

"Further evidence of the Banach–Tarski paradox"

I like bikes. And jam. And emergent French feminist discourse. Funky man, 51. Box no. 0559.

Labour power has only adopted the subjective conditions of necessary labour-subsistence indispensable for productive labour power. Tell that to a woman hungry for love and a free market economy. Box no. 0121.

The pin number for my credit card is 1917, my Facebook password is Trotsky, my hotmail secret question is 'Who replaced Julie Christie in the sequel to *A for Andromeda, The Andromeda Breakthrough?*' Camp, revolutionary social networking retro sci-fi geek (M, 43) WLTM similar for evenings dissecting Marx, the finer subplots of *Space: 1999* and the chagrin bag holding lurkers of *I Will Go Slightly Out Of My Way To Step On That Crunchy Looking Leaf*.[75] Wilts. No pervs. Box no. 8630.

I don't make cereal for anyone else. No Frills[76] biophysicist (learn the lingo and win my heart) WLTM dangerous tank-top wearing chemist for nights amongst the Petri-dishes and breakfast in the allergy lab (F, 35). Box no. 9703.

---

75 *A for Andromeda* (1961) – BBC TV science fiction drama written by cosmologist Fred Hoyle. It provided Julie Christie with her first major role. She was replaced by Susan Hampshire in the follow-up series, *The Andromeda Breakthrough*. *Space: 1999* (1975–77), UK science fiction series produced by Jerry and Sylvia Anderson, starring Martin Landau and Barbara Bain. *I Will Go Slightly Out Of My Way To Step On That Crunchy Looking Leaf* – member group on the social networking website Facebook.

76 No Frills – cheap, generic own-brand goods sold by the now defunct Kwik Save chain of supermarkets. The supermarket went into administration in 2007.

World's worst univocalic personal ad writer.[77] Male. 43. Box no. 9711.

Changes in fashion are only subordinate aspects of change. Trust me – I shop at Primark.[78] Off-the-peg feminist, darling of the red-dot sales: one size fits all but make it a delicate wash, and iron on reverse side only. WLTM baggy-fleeced male reader with some knowledge of continental sizes. Box no. 0523.

This advert is further evidence of the Banach–Tarski paradox.[79] Equidecomposable man, 43, currently existing in two subsets of Euclidean space. Cut this ad up and reassemble it into two of exactly the same idiocy. Not quite worked out yet how to talk to a woman without her 'going to make a phone call' and subsequently making her escape through the bathroom window. Would appreciate theorems and schematics explaining why. Box no. 6951.

This advert is my entry to the LRB's young person essay writing contest. I won't win it, however, because it is far too clever by half and also because I'm 62. Man, 62. Far too clever by half. Box no. 8887.

What are the chances? 1 in 216, as Richard de Fournival astutely explained in *De vetula*, written between 1220 and

---

77 Univocalic – consisting of only one vowel.

78 (See p. 55, n. 47.)

79 Theory proposed by Stefan Banach and Alfred Tarski in a paper published in 1924 that a ball can be decomposed into a finite number of point sets and reassembled into two balls identical to the original. Thus, the theory suggests that the points inside a pea can be sorted into pieces, and these pieces can then be rotated and reassembled to cover all the points of the sun.

1250.[80] I don't expect you to know that, however, because you're an idiot. Maths professor, 58, not afraid of being absolutely right at box no. 7765.

. . . .

I'm not Edith Wharton, but then this isn't the Riviera. Get real in Brighton with grey bombshell of the amusement arcades (43). Men with passion for Frogger, Donkey Kong and Antonin Artaud write to box no. 9702.[81]

. . . .

I went to university to learn how to write ads like this. Woman, 32. Box no. 4429.

. . . .

What you gonna do with all that junk? All that junk inside your trunk?[82] I'm gonna get a PhD in Social Sciences and spend Saturday nights alone in Oxted. Desperate woman, 34, all too aware of the misery caused by poor decision-making processes but more than willing to share it with men who don't have high sexual expectations and enjoy

. . . .

80   Richard de Fournival or Richart de Fornival (circa 1201–60) was a medieval philosopher and trouvère perhaps best known for the *Bestiaire d'Amour* (*Bestiary of Love*). *De vetula* is de Fournival's Latin poem offering a systematic study of the number of ways you can obtain any given total from a throw of three dice.

81   Edith Wharton (1862–1937) – American novelist, short-story writer, and essayist on architectural design. Frogger and Donkey Kong – arcade games that both made their debuts in 1981. Antonin Artaud (1896–1948) – French playwright, poet, actor, and director.

82   Taken from the song 'My Humps', written by will.i.am and D. Payton. Performed by Black Eyed Peas and taken from their album *Monkey Business* (2005, A&M/Interscope). The song reached number three in both the US and UK charts. It was the subject of intense music press criticism upon its release. John Bush, writing in *All Music Guide*, described it as 'one of the most embarrassing rap performances of the new millennium', and Bill Lamb, writing for *About.com*, called it 'the musical equivalent of a bad Farrelly Brothers movie'. Hua Hsu of *Slate.com* said, 'It's not Awesomely Bad; it's Horrifically Bad. . . . There are bad songs that offend our sensibilities but can still be enjoyed, and then there are the songs that are just really bad – transcendentally bad, objectively bad.' A poll conducted by *Rolling Stone* ranked the song first in the list of 20 most annoying songs.

any female company that isn't their mother (which, I'm guessing, pretty much covers most of the male readership of this magazine). Box no. 8820.

March 1993. I was the third member of the Ricketts Family on *Family Fortunes* (related by marriage, now divorced). Name a vegetable you would serve with a Sunday roast. I said Butternut Squash, sliced and gently cooked in olive oil, but the survey of one hundred of Britain's dullest peasant yokels didn't. I may not have been able to share a brand new Polo hatchback with the nation's most barbarous and uncultured family, but I think I made my point. Who's laughing now, Les Dennis?[83] Man, 38, lecturer at UCL. Box no. 2213.

Apparently the Three Symmedians aren't a novelty Bosnian folk troupe.[84] Rubbish mathematician (M, 37). Box no. 2695.

Woman keen to get a birthday card from significant other this year (it's in August, you've got plenty of time) WLTM Gottfried Wilhelm Leibniz-type man to 50 just to be on the safe side.[85] Box no. 5257.

The Necker cube of personal ads[86] – are you viewing

---

83 *Family Fortunes* – television game show based on the US show *Family Feud*. The show ran from 1979 to 2002, revived again in 2006. Les Dennis (b. 1954) was the show's host between 1987 and 2002.

84 Symmedian – one of three geometrical lines intersecting in a single point (the symmedian) on a triangle.

85 Gottfried Wilhelm Leibniz (1646–1716) – German polymath and the discoverer of the binary numeral system in which numeric values are represented by two digits (commonly 0 and 1).

86 Necker cube – an optical illusion first published in 1832 by Swiss crystallographer Louis Albert Necker. A wire-frame drawing of a cube in

from above or below? Irritating amateur psychologist (M, 52) seeks woman with brain suitable for home-made experiments. Half-full/half-empty relationship and psychometric tests a-plenty at box no. 5447.

Not only will this advert win me the woman of my dreams (25, tall, brunette, fun, likes late nights, computer games and Pop Tarts), it also wins me a place at the grown-ups' table. Errant son, 18, swapping Dad's *Hustler*[87] subscription for this crap for the last two years. Box no. 0530.

These are my skills: I can swim five lengths, I know karate (I used to be a yellow belt), I can roll my eyelids back, I can do an impression of Wally from *Crossroads*,[88] I can run really fast when I'm being chased, I can make awesome tracks on my Casio keyboard, I was in a shop in Croydon once and there was a gap in one of the dressing room curtains and you could see in and Christine Rowley was inside trying some stuff on and I saw one of her boobs. Man, 38. Senior Philosophy lecturer. Box no. 9920.

isometric perspective, the Necker cube can be interpreted in two different (although both seemingly correct) ways, alternating which side can be interpreted as the front/reverse of the cube. The illusion helps form an understanding of the human visual system and of the human brain being a neural network with two distinct and interchangeable stable states.

87   *Hustler* – monthly pornographic magazine first published in the US in 1974.

88   The reference here may be to the 1996 song 'The Crossroads' by Cleveland hip-hop group Bone Thugs-N-Harmony, which originally contained the line 'And, Wally, even though you're gone, you've still got love from bone' although it's much more likely that the advertiser is citing the television soap opera *Crossroads*, set in a motel near Birmingham. It was originally broadcast on the ITV network between 1964 and 1988 before being revised briefly in 2003. Wally Sopper was a peripheral character in the soap, fond of concocting abstruse money-making schemes. He appeared in the series during the early to mid-eighties.

The Schrödinger's cat of personal ads.[89] Box no. 3611.

The original C&A man.[90] One day polyester will return, and then I will rule you all. Princess in peachy nylon twist needed to sit beside throne of lecturer in comparative studies, 37, London. Box no. 7997.

An inspired calligrapher can create pages of beauty using stick ink, quill, brush, pick-axe, buzz saw, or even strawberry jam. Pangrams[91] of delight, but the worst sex you've ever had with dumpy kibitzer (M, 41) jingling as exchequer overflows at box no. 9791.

89 Thought experiment devised by Austrian physicist Erwin Schrödinger around 1935. In it, Schrödinger attempted to illustrate what he saw as the problems of the Copenhagen interpretation of quantum mechanics when it is applied beyond atomic or subatomic systems. The experiment proposes that a live cat be placed in a hermetically sealed steel chamber, along with a device containing a vial of hydrocyanic acid. Also in the chamber is a small amount of a radioactive substance. If an atom of the substance decays, a relay mechanism trips the hammer, breaking the vial and killing the cat. The observer cannot know whether or not any decay of the substance has occurred, and therefore cannot know whether the vial has been broken, the acid released, and the cat killed. Thus, according to quantum law, the cat is both alive and dead in a superposition of states. Only upon opening the box does the observer learn the condition of the cat. However, in doing so, the superposition is lost and the cat becomes either alive or dead. The observation or measurement itself affects an outcome and the outcome does not exist unless the observation is made. This is sometimes referred to as 'quantum indeterminacy'.

90 C&A – international chain store selling budget clothing. Founded in the Netherlands in 1861 as a textile company by brothers Clemens and August Brenninkmeijer. The store ceased trading in the UK in 2001 but continues to trade elsewhere in the world.

91 Pangram – a sentence that uses every letter of the alphabet at least once. The advertiser here has constructed two pangrams.

This personal advert completely debunks Hooke's Law of elasticity.[92] This, and other laws of physics turned upside down (did you know light doesn't travel in waves, but in packs?) by amateur dentist (M, 38). Box no. 7267.

I was born to write this advert. Biologist M, 43. 15 years spent researching necrotizing fasciitis (fasciitis necroticans)[93] would really, really, really like a girlfriend. Box no. 7543.

0011001100110001000IOIIOIOIIIIOOIOIIOOIOIOIIOOOOIOIII
OOIOOOIOOOOOOIIOIIIIOIIOIIOOOIIOOIOOOOIOOOOOOIIOOOI
IOIIOIIIOIIOIIOIOIIIOOOOOIIOIOIOIOIIIOIOOOIIOIOOIOIIO
IIIOOIIOOIIIOOIOOOOOOIIOOIIIOIIOOIOIOIIOOIOIOIIOIOII
OOIOOOOOOIIIOOIIOIIOOIOIOIIOOIOIOIIOIOIIOIIIOOIIOOIO
OOOOIIOIIIIOIIIOOOOOIIOOIOIOIIOIIIOOOIOIIOIOIIOIIOI
OIIOIOOIOIIOIIIOOIIOOIOOOIIOOIOIOIIOOIOOOOIOOOOOOII
OOOIOOIIOIIOOOIIOIIIIOIIOIIIOOIIOOIOOOIIOOIOIOOIOOOO
OOIIIOIOOOIIIOIIIOIIOIOIOIOIIOIIIOOIIIOOIIOOIOOOOOOIII
OOIIOIIOIOOIOIIIOOIIOIIIOIOOOIIOOIOIOIIOOIOOIIIOOIIO
OIOOOOOOIIIOIIIOIIOIOIOOIOIIIOIOOOIIOIOOOOOIOOOOOOIII
OIIOOIIOOIOIOIIIOOIOOIIIIOOIOOIOOOOOOIIOIIOOOIIOOOO
IOIIIOOIOOIIOOIIOIIOOIOIOOIOOOOOOIIOOOIOOIIIOOIOOII
OOIOIOIIOOOOIOIIIOOIIOIIOIOIOOOIIIOOIIOOIOIIIOOOIOOOO
OOIOOIIIIOIIIOIIOIIOIIOIIOOOIOOOOOOIIOIIOIOIIOOOOIOII
OIIIOOIIOOIIOIIOIOOIOIIOIIIIOIIOIIIOOOIOOOOOOIIIOIII
OIIOIOOIOIIIOIOOOIIOIOOOOOIOOOOOOOIOOOOOOIIIOOOOOI
IOIIIIOIIOIIIOIIOIIOOOOIOOOOOOIIOOOOIOIIOIIIOOOIOOO
OOOIIOOOOIOIIOOIOOOIIIOIIOOIIOOOOIOIIOIIIOOIIIOIOOOI

92   Hooke's Law – named after the seventeenth-century physicist Robert Hooke and first stated in 1676 as a Latin anagram. Hooke published the solution in 1678 'Ut tensio, sic vis', meaning 'As the extension, so the force.' In other words, the amount by which a material body is deformed is linearly related to the force causing the deformation.

93   Flesh-eating bacteria.

10000101100111011100101 and must have keen knowledge of binary systems.[94] Box no. 2318.

....

Easily-distracted cytogeneticist (F, 53) seeks anyone capable of enacting quinacrine banding during their turn at charades. Is it a book? A film? A song? No – it's a mitotic inhibitor being added to a cell culture.[95] Please hold me. Box no. 6838.

....

Subscribed for the crossword. And the funnies. Sorely disappointed LRB reader (F, 36), yet to get one laugh out of Perry Anderson, or a workable anagram out of Slavoj Žižek.[96] WLTM dumbed-down man to 45 who starts at the personals and then gives up. Box no. 1010.

....

My Weltanschauung[97] informs me there are plenty of losers in this column but very few winners. It also tells me there is possibly one dentist and a smithy, neither of whom are me. I'm a lecturer in media studies. But if you are the dentist or smithy, or if you're friends with either of them, why not write? M, 47. Mancs. Box no. 0221.

....

94   (See p. 88, n. 85.) The binary in this advert translates as '32-year old computing geek seeks open-minded blonde twin sisters with very large breasts. Own mansion with pool an advantage'.

95   Cytogenetics is the study of the structure and function of the cell, particularly chromosomes. Banding is a technique used to produce a visible karyotype by staining condensed chromosomes. Quinacrine banding (Q-banding) was the first staining method of banding used in cytogenetics and is done using the antiprotozoal drug quinacrine. Mitotic inhibitors are used during slide preparation to stop cell division and thereby increase the number of mitotic cells available for analysis.

96   Perry Anderson (b. 1938) – historian, essayist and author. Slavoj Žižek (b. 1949) – cultural critic. Both are regular contributors to the *London Review of Books*.

97   Weltanschauung – German philosophical concept of a world view, or wide world perception.

Latka Gravas of the Humanities concourse (male, 31): real-time bathos, basic knowledge of spanners, and a finely-tuned slapstick instinct. A. J. P. Taylor will never read the same again.[98] Box no. 0531.

Sorry is not the hardest word – auscultatory is. And bouzouki. Lexicographical gymnast (retired, M, 40), WLTM woman willing to easily concede defeat at Scrabble.[99] Berks. Box no. 0917.

English lecturer, 44. Modelling himself on The Fonz in an entirely non-ironic way since 1979.[100] Box no. 5222.

[98] Latka Gravas – fictional character from the ABC television sitcom *Taxi* (1978–82) portrayed by Andy Kaufman. Latka was based on a character Kaufman created known as 'Foreign Man'. A. J. P. Taylor – Alan John Percivale Taylor (1906–90), influential historian born in Birkdale, Merseyside.

[99] Auscultatory – of or pertaining to auscultation, or listening to the sounds of the body. Bouzouki – a stringed Greek and Balkan folk instrument. Assuming no triple word scores, or double letter scores, 'auscultatory' would score 17 in a game of Scrabble, whereas 'bouzouki' would score 23. 'Sorry' would score 8.

[100] Arthur Herbert Fonzarelli (also known as the Fonz or simply Fonzie) – a fictional character played by Henry Winkler in the US sitcom *Happy Days* (see p. 22, n. 11).

"The Skomorokh of Gender Confusion"

If you don't believe an evening in my company will be
entertaining enough, just come and spend fifteen minutes
with me and my personal wizard. Gaze in amazement
as the archimage alters your perception of reality and
awakens you to a world of many colours and sensations.
Gurgle in delight as his top hat becomes a haven for
the creatures of the Secret Forest. Bark in disgust as his
linking rings become entangled in his hidden trouser
compartment. M, 54, Tamworth. No time wasters. Box no.
7388.

Stop with all the small talk. I've a full tub of margarine
and a set of Yahtzee dice with your name on them. The
Jenga's at my place, but first, Newsnight. Man, 47. Box no.
1119.

I am the only piece of eye-candy appearing in this
column. You are the only comely dentist. Are we fools to
think it could ever work? Maths-obsessed cross-dressing
M in Manolo Blahniks and Prada A-lines seeks health-food
fascist and mismatched Oxfam disaster to 50 for long
division, bursts of real fruit flavour and evenings worrying
about the sugar-content of M&S slightly soileds. No
barristers. Box no. 8631.

If I wear a mask, will you call me Batman? Just asking. Box
no. 0558.

Former Miss World[101] sought by trainee old perv (76). Box
no. 6440.

---

[101] See appendix.

Leave me alone with your father for an evening and by the end of the night we'll have gotten drunk together, have nicknames for each other and be scheduling in a football game. Give me the weekend and we'll be lovers. Man in denial, 35, determined to bring everyone you know out of the closet before crawling into it himself and nailing the door shut from the inside. Box no. 7509.

The eyes said 'take me, I'm yours': the thighs said 'pre-operative; and it's a long waiting list'. Why doth thou mock me, oh ye Gods? M, 42. Box no. 0216.

A night with me is like a night at the Playboy Mansion.[102] Tony (48), Bridgend. Box no. 3339.

The Harlequin of Doubt has visited me more than once. Often he is accompanied by the Jester of Shame. Either of these, however, is preferable to the Skomorokh of Gender Confusion, who comes whenever mother leaves me alone in the house. Divorced chemist, M, 53. Box no. 7789.

Some men can only be loved by their own mother. Not me, I've got Mr Snugly Panda. Male, 36, and Mr Snugly Panda, also 36. Box no. 9912.

I'm still Jenny from the block.[103] Which is odd because yesterday I was Keith from the allotment. Keith from the allotment, 49. You can call me Jenny. Box no. 6411.

---

102   10236 Charing Cross Rd., Holmby Hills, Los Angeles, California, 90024. The original Playboy Mansion was at 1340 N. State Parkway, Chicago, Illinois, 60610. As such, the current Playboy Mansion is often known as Playboy Mansion West.

103   'Jenny from the Block' – written by Andre 'mrDEYO' Deyo, Jennifer Lopez, Jean Claude 'Poke' Olivier, Samuel Barnes, Lawrence Parker, Simon Sterlin, and Jose Fernando Arbex Miro. Performed by Jennifer Lopez and taken

Three years ago I'd have doubted that I'd ever have the guts to place a lonely-heart advertising for an attractive, intelligent man to 54. But then three years ago I was wearing work-site boots and doubted that I'd ever go through with the breast enhancement surgery and oestrogen injections. My confidence as a woman grows daily, but my taste in footwear is still determinedly health and safety conscious at box no. 8911.

I have 39 years of magical experiences behind me. Gay epicurean land registrar and flamenco dancer (M). Box no. 6825.

I'd like to thank all the women of the LRB who have taken the time to read this advert by making love to you all. Honestly, it's the least I could do. Extremely grateful gentleman (76, but my tiny Elvis still works). Box no. 4311.

38 years of non-stop sitting and snacking may have taken their toll on my waistline, arteries and kidney functions, but this libido is as active as it ever was (think John Holmes in a mu'umu'u).[104] Man. Leicester. A bit

from her album *This Is Me . . . Then* (2002, Epic). Reached number three in the *Billboard* Hot 100. The song is one of a growing number where the theme juxtaposes the performer's upbringing with their celebrity status. In Lopez's case, her childhood in the Bronx, New York, is juxtaposed with her paparazzi-haunted life as a successful performer and girlfriend of Hollywood movie actor Ben Affleck. The chorus includes the lines 'Don't be fooled by the rocks that I got / I'm still, I'm still Jenny from the block'. Other songs following a similar theme are Faith Hill's 'Mississippi Girl' (2005), Gwen Stefani's 'Orange County Girl' (2007) and Fergie's 'Glamorous' (2007).

104 John Holmes (1944–88) – pornographic actor, also known as John C. Holmes or Johnny Wadd. One of the most recognizable male adult film stars of all time, Holmes appeared in approximately 2,500 pornographic features (movies, adult loops and stag films) in the 1970s and 1980s, including at least one gay feature film and a small number of gay loops. He was best known for his exceptionally large penis, which was marketed as being the largest in the

clammy but all smiles and busy, busy hands at box no. 8121.

A sexual renaissance compels me (tupinaire enthusiast, M, 56) to write this advert. Box no. 1710.

If there really was a god, Adam Phillips[105] would arrive and tell me these fantasies are healthy reactions to years spent in a cold, unforgiving and cruel marriage. Though I'm not sure mother would see it quite the same way. Is it too much, too soon? Hello? Box no. 2221.

Apparently BBW is not a type of post-doctoral qualification.[106] Eight-stone male dufus (42) seeks urgent help with redefining most of his life's assumptions. Box no. 5311.

Women to 35 – you're all invited to the party in my pants. It's bring your own bottle and, please, remember to

porn industry (its exact dimensions are unknown, although both his first wife, Sharon Gebenini, and his last wife, Laurie 'Misty Dawn' Rose, both stated that Holmes himself claimed his penis was ten inches long, although Holmes' incessant self-promotion often led him to claim it was as large as fourteen inches. Porn actress Annette Haven, however, has stated that Holmes never achieved a full erection, 'It was like doing it with a big, soft kind of loofah'). Holmes also attracted notoriety for his involvement in the brutal Wonderland Murders in 1981, when four people were killed in a drug-related plot allegedly masterminded by businessman and drug dealer Eddie Nash. Holmes died from an AIDS-related illness in 1988 and was the inspiration for two Hollywood movies, *Boogie Nights* (1997, dir. Paul Thomas Anderson) and *Wonderland* (2003, dir. James Cox). Mu'umu'u – loose, traditionally Hawaiian dress popular as maternity gowns.

105   Adam Phillips (b. 1954) – psychotherapist, essayist, and author.

106   Acronym meaning 'Big Beautiful Woman'. The phrase and its acronym were coined by Carole Shaw in 1979, when she launched *BBW Magazine*, a fashion and lifestyle magazine for plus-size women. 'BBW' is often used in personal ads and fetish websites.

remove your shoes before you step on the carpet – mum's just had it cleaned. Stupid man, 33. Box no. 7010.

9.30 Night of a Thousand Shows; 10.15 BBC News; 10.30 Have I Got 2001 News for You; 11.15 It's Your New Year's Eve Party; 12.20am Are You Being Served?; 12.21 Insane Tantric Sex Bent Backwards Over a Decade's Worth of National Geographic. Finally, a New Year's Eve worth staying up for. Bolton night-school teacher (M, 38, likes cocoa before, after, and – if you're lucky – during). Athletic women, please, write to box no. 9118.

You're so vain. I bet you think this ad is about you. Don't you? Don't you? You couldn't be more wrong. Unless you're a Carly Simon-loving nutcase with a collection of wide-brimmed floppy hats, espadrilles and every flavour of herbal tea stocked by Holland and Barrett. Simple man, 43, with simple tastes.[107] Box no. 7651.

Don't listen to your inner voice in matters of the heart! Especially if your inner voice tells you to check his outgoing message box for evidence of a wife or ask why he always needs to be on the last train to Stafford instead

---

107 'You're So Vain' – written and performed by Carly Simon. Taken from her album No Secrets (1972, Elektra Records). It reached number one in the Billboard Hot 100. Since its release, the song has been the subject of intense speculation as to who the subject is. In 2003, the head of NBC Sports, Dick Ebersol, paid $50,000 at a charity auction to learn of the identity of the song's subject. The condition of winning the auction was that he wasn't allowed to reveal the identity to anyone else, save for one letter, 'E'. Simon herself later added the letters 'A' and 'R' as clues, which made Mick Jagger, Warren Beatty and James Taylor the main candidates (Simon had relationships with all three). Although she was married to Taylor shortly before the song was written, she has stated that the song isn't about him. Mick Jagger sang uncredited backing vocals on the song. In April 2007, Warren Beatty gave an interview to a US journalist in which he said, 'Let's be honest. That song was about me.'

of just staying the night. It's a simple rule, but it's a rule that will give us many happy – if somewhat opprobrious – experiences together. Man, 38. Not in the slightest bit married. Remember that. Box no. 4329.

There's something about austere cleanliness that makes my sex engine purr like a kitten. Man, 37, could possibly attract a woman if only I could think of better openers. Box no. 2213.

"Blast into a future of love"

Capricorn Fifteens. Born 2244. Enter the Carousel. This is the time of renewal. Re-enacting *Logan's Run* in the corridors of UCL – history lecturer WLTM woman to 45 for whom the phrase 'be strong and you will be renewed' is often a prelude to intercourse.[108] Box no. 6936.

The genre-crossing personal ad. It begins as Romance with this mention of Jane Austen, before turning into Contemporary Fiction with this reference to the latest Thomas Pynchon novel. But once we meet it's all Sci-Fi as I persuade you (and I will – my argument is perfectly sound and very coherently structured) about the existence of extra-terrestrials who walk amongst us disguised as doctors, academics, lawyers, my ex-wife and, latterly, following an absurd three-month 'cooling-off' restraining order, my probation officer. Man, 48. Warwick. Box no. 3222. The truth is out there.

Puny Earthlings! I am come to bring a reign of terror upon your intellectually inferior world for a period not less than a thousand years of dark, impenetrable night! Women-folk – I'm going to have to ask you to remove your shirts and send photos to would-be Mekon, 43, sleeping on his sister's sofa the last three months running.[109] Box no. 9733.

This advert is my best attempt at adequately expressing the true nature of the 46-year old man who placed it. It

---

108 *Logan's Run* (1976, dir. Michael Anderson) – film based on the dystopian novel of the same name by William F. Nolan and George Clayton Johnson, in which the population is controlled by killing people as they reach the age of thirty ('the time of renewal').

109 Mekon – ruler of the Treens and arch-enemy of Dan Dare.

may look unremarkable but, given the scant dimensions humans are aware of, it's nothing short of miraculous. Reply now and I will show you how it reads among the peaceful Drivulian dream swimmers that populate our minds at night. Box no. 4740.

Man ahead of his time (aged 328 of your earth years). Join me in my Chiswick time machine and together we can blast into a future of love, lust and microwaveable trousers. Box no. 1007.

World of the Strange! LRB reader (F, then 36) places personal advert in 2001 for man to 40 who loves literature, the arts and cycling in Italy. She receives no responses whatsoever but duly notes over the course of the next five years the number of male advertisers to 40 appearing in the same publication who enjoy literature, the arts and cycling in Italy (there were thirteen of them). Is the reason they didn't reply to her advert because they were blind to her outrageous beauty or because she lived in a house in which an old soldier had died upon returning from the Great War in 1918 and had subsequently cursed all future inhabitants, preventing them from ever being happy (this same curse also prevents inhabitants of the house from being able to make omelettes or perform basic house chores such as washing dishes and opening utility bills)? F, now 41, believes it to be the latter and WLTM M to 45 with some knowledge of exorcism rituals, direct debits and the best place for bulk paper plate purchases. Box no. 4784.

You like walking barefoot on cold beaches in the winter, movies that make you cry and baking cookies that you have no intention of eating. I like defending my home against the government forces that are trying to destroy me and knitting carpet samples from fibre remnants found in the back of the dryers at my local launderette. Are we fools to think it could ever work? Moron and amateur carpet sample enthusiast (M, 35). Box no. 5331.

When the authorities eventually remove this covert recording device from my brain, they'll be able to download not only the most profound musings on the universe ever conceived by man but also possibly the whereabouts of my car keys. Until then paranoid amateur tailor (M, 37, Warwickshire) remains unable to take these cross-stitch manuals back to the library. The chirps and whistles aren't getting any quieter, and the fines aren't getting any smaller, but this dog-fur suit is sewing up a storm at box no. 4476. That's not revulsion you're feeling right now – it's passion (or possibly it is revulsion).

Consult the spirits to measure our compatibility:

YES   NO

A B C D E F G H I J K L M
N O P Q R S T U V W X Y Z
1 2 3 4 5 6 7 8 9 0

Goodbye

Box no. 8511.

This personal advert contains more than one hypnotic suggestion. Box no. 7637.

Superheroes of BMX – join me (fortean beast-hunter, M, 34) in my quest for the Cannock Crocodile and help me make Staffordshire as safe a place for geese as ever there was. Or else just hold me and stroke my hair.[110] Box no. 4324.

Two heads are better than one! Amateur geneticist and dancing fool (M, 48 and two months) seeks woman to 46 willing to sign an affidavit promising not to reveal the secrets of patent-pending Mind Splicing Machine™ to the scientific community at large. Own apron, gloves and machine that makes whizzy noises a distinct advantage. Box no. 6790.

When the Antmen unite, all will be their slaves. Man, 46, WLTM woman to 50 for whom this opening line works as a proem to sex. Box no. 6222.

By reading this advert you have unwittingly become the latest in my mind experiments in which I persuade the subject to believe I'm a 6'1", sandy blonde Abercrombie & Fitch model[111] with the world at my feet and a lifetime

---

110 'Superheroes of BMX' – written and performed by Mogwai. Taken from their album 4 *Satin* (1997, Chemikal Underground, Jetset). Cannock Crocodile – in June 2003, the Staffordshire town of Cannock (population: 92,500) was put on alert after numerous sightings of a crocodile loose in the local Roman View Pond. An investigation by the RSPCA led to the capture of a snapper turtle (later nicknamed 'lucky') although the cryptozoologist group CFZ (Centre for Fortean Zoology, based in Bideford, north Devon) concluded in a field study report shortly after the RSPCA investigation that the size of the beast in the sightings (estimated at between three and five feet in length) was far too large to be a snapper turtle.

111 Abercrombie & Fitch – US lifestyle clothing brand specializing in casual luxury apparel for the early-twenties market. The model referred to in the advert could be Matt Ratliff, who is 6'1" and was chosen to represent the archetype of the A&F blonde-haired, sporty, youthful male consumer in many campaigns following his arrival to the A&F brand as the main face of their Christmas 2005 campaign.

of excitement ahead of me. Man, 57. 6′1″, sandy blonde
Abercrombie & Fitch model with the world at my feet and a
lifetime of excitement ahead of me. Worthing. Box no. 9117.

The only name listed under my old school on
FriendsReunited[112] is mine. That's because I was taught at
home in an isolated farmhouse, far from the shrieking hordes
of bird-men that mummy said circled the town, and where I
learned how to write by tracing the letters of Dean Friedman
lyrics. You'd be welcome in my home anytime (M, 41) but don't
tell mummy that you want to leave. Box no. 6338.

My favourite Thundercat was Cheetara, and that's the
way I see you: hand-activated bo-staff, accurate – though
limited – application of a psychic sixth sense and fastest of
the clowder.[113] Idiot man, 34. Box no. 9844.

Forward this personal ad to ten friends. Otherwise bad
luck will befall you. Poison pen lady (32, Staffs). Box no.
4675.

Are you planning on crossing the road after reading this?
Beware – spy cameras on distant satellites watch your every
move, looking for changing heat patterns on the tarmac.
Join my campaign to bring back telephoto-resistant
cobbles at box no. 0416. (Man, 38.)

I intend to keep the precise contents of this personal ad
secret. Box no. 5722.

112   FriendsReunited.co.uk – online service aimed at reuniting old school
friends, family members, work colleagues, etc. Dean Friedman, see p. 25, n. 17.

113   *Thundercats* – US animated television series running between 1985 and
1990, following the adventures of a group of cat-like humanoids from the dead
planet Thundera. Cheetara was the only adult female of the group until the
appearance of Pumyra after several seasons.

As it happens, 11.34am two weeks next Friday is the first day of the rest of my life. Nuclear physicist (M, 40) on the brink of time-travelling break-through. Write now to box no. 9859 but be aware that by the time I reply you will be 98 whereas I will have aged just twelve hours. You may have a good-looking grand-daughter by then though. Give her my number and tell her to look me up.

Watch out! Not all sausage rolls are free of eavesdropping microchips. Be safe by rubbing all shop-bought pastries with a strong magnet. Then write to Oxford hick (F), thirties, at box no. 0560.

I used to watch a lot of TV. Now I just sit in my chair and watch the lights come through the keyhole and make crazy, crazy patterns on the wall. M UFO abductee WLT re-establish contact with the others (esp. 'Jenny'). Box no. 2385.

"Forty years ago I was going to marry Elvis"

Catterick Ladies' Circle. I don't want to meet on Tuesday mornings anymore. I don't want to take the dictation for Kate's obituary notice in the paper. I don't want to start the Christmas lights petition. I really don't like golf – I don't understand it and all that waiting around hurts my knees. I don't want my photograph taken with you all for the local paper, celebrating our 'fun walk' for the blind. I don't want a video intercom installed to 'make me feel more secure' – it's not really like the Bronx here just yet. I know all about the benefits of a high fibre diet – please don't make me listen to the man from the well-woman clinic giving a talk about it. I'm glad that the grandchildren never visit; they smell and have terrible manners. I know you all mean well – but I want to behave inappropriately with a man half my age and be the rumour that opens the meeting I'll be absent from next Tuesday morning. Box no. 6901.

When love eludes you, try provincial living! Gorgeous, ersatz fem (34) living the self-sufficiency dream seeks strong-armed, bold man to 40 to make only positive comments about her needlepoint work and help churn the butter daily. Must have working knowledge of calf-birthing procedures. Box no. 9761.

If a break-up to you means spending most lunchtimes crying over chicken skewers at All Bar One then join me, big-boned F (37), and we can share a World Tapas bundle dish and save ourselves a fortune. Afterwards we can make love, but not before the chocolate fondant dessert. I can be found at the Henrietta Street branch, Wednesdays between 12 and 2, requesting fries with my hoi sin duck quesadilla. Box no. 4290.

One day I'll edit this magazine. Then maybe I'll be able to get my direct debit cancelled. Until then I'll take whatever I can get (F, 34). Box no. 1299.

Forty years ago I was going to marry Elvis – at 56 my expectations are lower. The least you could do is try to meet them. If you're over 4′10″, it's a start. Box no. 1210.

No beards. F, 38. Box no. 6956.

Does anyone read these ads? Apart from my mother, I mean? If so, write to beautiful, vivacious, intelligent Jewish F (34) who won't spend every dinner comparing you to her ex-boyfriend. I make no such guarantees about my mother though (hi, mum). Box no. 2511.

Newly divorced man, 46, looking for a woman to 50 who doesn't conclude sexual intercourse with Queen Katherine's rebuke to Cardinal Wolsey.[114] Box no. 6531.

Hazlewood seeks Sinatra; Presley seeks Ann-Margret; Kristofferson seeks Coolidge; Chiswick Jackie Chan seeks any sort of unmusical, vague, ambiguous, shoehorned love interest of no particular narrative consequence. Help me make it through the chorus only at box no. 1717.[115]

---

114 'I do believe, induced by potent circumstances, that thou art mine enemy' – from Shakespeare's *Henry VIII*, II, iv.

115 Lee Hazlewood often sang with Nancy Sinatra. Elvis Presley began a brief, much gossiped-about affair with Ann-Margret in 1964. Kris Kristofferson was married to Rita Coolidge from 1973 to 1980. Jackie Chan is a martial arts actor. The final line of the advert is taken from Kristofferson's 'Help Me Make It Through the Night' (written and performed by Kris Kristofferson), from his album *Kristofferson* (1970, Monument).

I wish they all could be Californian,[116] but basically anyone within the M25 will do. Man, 43. No criteria beyond the limits of the London Underground network. Oh, and a D-cup. Box no. 1009.

My last husband was a loser. If you're not a loser please reply. Woman, 40. Incredibly simple criteria. Box no. 4356.

I've written every advert that's ever appeared in this column, but I've written them with tears. And pain. And sometimes Tizer. And Quavers. And, last week, baked beans crushed onto the end of a comb. Woman, 32, WLTM man with collection of working pens. Functional penis also a distinct advantage. Box no. 6886.

This is positively your last chance to find love. Unless they place this ad somewhere in the middle of the column. Box no. 0526.

When replying to this ad, please specify which type of beverage I should excessively consume before we meet. Woman, 46. Far too used to the standard of LRB-reading men this column throws up yet now prone to migraines caused by red wine where red wine used to make self-hating first date sex so much more bearable. Baileys-types are a definite no-no (I get a yeast reaction to dairy). Box no. 6792.

---

116 Presumed to be taken from the Beach Boys' song 'California Girls', written by Mike Love and Brian Wilson. Performed by The Beach Boys and taken from the album *Summer Days (And Summer Nights!!)* (1965, Capitol). Reached number three in the *Billboard* Hot 100 charts. Written immediately after he had taken LSD for the first time, Wilson claimed that the same LSD experience also created a permanent threatening voice in his head that would eventually lead to his mental illness later in life.

My ideal man is King Gustavus Adolphus of Sweden.[117] But as long as you don't leave the door open during toilet moments and adopt the so-called 'eco-friendly' maxim 'if it's yellow, let it mellow' then you'll do. Historian F, 37. Has long since learned not to expect much from this column, but would like a guy who flushes. Box no. 2231.

There comes a point in most intellectual women's lives when they realise that, as attractive and intelligent as they may be, the LRB is not the place to find an energetic, cultured, good-looking man. Hell, it's not even the place to find a guy who doesn't begin his conversations with 'the biopsy revealed nothing – but I swear there's something not right down there'. This advert, therefore, is less a last ditch attempt to be proven wrong, and more a 'so long, suckers' to all the other women still reading this column when they could dumb down to the Guardian Soulmates and taste long-forgotten fruit. Come on in, girls, the water's lovely – even if the water's full of spelling mistakes, author interviews that no one gives a crap about, and stuff lifted from the previous night's Evening Standard. Box no. 8810.

LRB on-line RPG[118] **nerds:** you are the most wretched group of bores to exist on God's good earth. Never reply to me. Never, never, never. Previously affable, now largely intolerant and recently divorced woman (34)

---

117   King Gustav II Adolf (1594–1632) – in Swedish, Gustav Adolf den Store. Founder of the Swedish Empire, he lead the Swedish armies as king from the age of seventeen until his death on the battlefield in 1632 during the Thirty Years War.

118   Role-playing games. The advertiser is possibly referring to *World of Warcraft*, the fourth game set in the American computer game developers Blizzard Entertainment's *Warcraft* multi-player online gaming universe. The game was designed by Rob Pardo, Jeff Kaplan, and Tom Chilton and released

WLTM a bloke my age who doesn't spend 15 hours a day pretending he's a heroic blacksmith killing stuff in some other-dimensional village resembling Cottingley, West Yorkshire, circa 1902. Talk to me, not Olaf the Destroyer, at box no. 3633.

Newly divorced man, 38, WLTM woman to 40 whose heroes don't include Leslie Cole, Bill 'Dink' Hewit, Roger Martinez, Peter Jaconelli, Dave Man or William Corfield.[119] Northumbria. Box no. 6362.

My last date resulting from an ad in this column didn't turn up because he'd been rushed to hospital having mixed two industrial cleaners whilst mopping his kitchen floor.

in November 2004 in celebration of the tenth anniversary of the first *Warcraft* game. Players can choose to be one of nine class of player: Druid, Hunter, Mage, Paladin, Priest, Rogue, Shaman, Warlock, or Warrior. The game has frequently been criticized for being addictive: in August 2005, the Chinese government proposed new rules to limit the time its estimated 20 million gamers spent daily playing online games in general, following a number of incidents including one where a gamer killed a fellow player who had stolen his virtual sword. *Wired. com* published an article in 2006 by digital entrepreneur and journalist Joichi Ito called 'World of Warcrack', in which he stated, 'I have never been this addicted to anything before. My other hobbies are gone . . . my social life revolves more and more around friends in the game'.

119   All former world record holders. Leslie Cole set the record for the fastest consumption of eels (1 pound of elvers in 43 seconds) at Frampton-on-Severn, Gloucestershire, on 13 April 1971. Bill 'Dink' Hewit set the record for fastest consumption of soft-boiled eggs (25 in three minutes, 1.8 seconds) in Bethlehem, Pennsylvania, on 2 October 1971. Roger Martinez ate 225 live goldfish (setting the record for most live goldfish consumed) at St Mary's University, San Antonio, Texas, on 6 February 1970. Councillor Peter Jaconelli, Mayor of Scarborough, Yorkshire, ate the most oysters in 60 minutes (500) at the Castle Hotel on 27 April 1972. Dave Man ate the most prunes in the fastest time (130, without pits, in 105 seconds) at Eastbourne, East Sussex, on 16 June 1971. William Corfield ate 81 unshelled whelks in 15 minutes at Helyar Arms, East Coker, Somerset, on 6 September 1969, though it isn't clear whether the record in this instance was for quantity, speed, or gastric resilience.

Thanks for nothing, LRB and Cillit Bang.[120] Women with tales of dating woe more agonizing than this please write to box no. 8753. I've given up on sex and now just need words of reassurance.

You'd have thought that this magazine would be fertile ground for the acquisition of cocktail party banter and intellectual snippets to chew over while sipping martinis. But I've been to LRB bookshop subscriber nights and can promise you it's not. Woman, 37, consuming all the free chardonnay by the poetry section in the basement. Bring your discount card, and an opening line that doesn't involve Ross McKibbin's latest piece, and I'll almost certainly sleep with you.[121] Box no. 7699.

Getting laid through Match.com[122] isn't as easy as the adverts make it out to be. I'm hoping for better pickings from this column. Woman, 87. Box no. 5444.

Obwohl sie eine erfolgreiche Investment-Bankerin war, war sie unzufrieden mit ihrem Leben. Irgendetwas fehlte. Sie versuchte all diese Stimmungen, Gedanken und Mythen die als Schranke zum Glück im Leben und in Beziehungen stehen, zu konfrontieren. Erfolg war definiert durch Geld, den perfekten Ehemann und Erfolg im Beruf. Und trotzdem, fragte sie sich, wer ist schon durch und durch glücklich? Alle Leute, die das alles erreicht haben, sind die wirklich glücklich? Ziemlich ahrscheinlich, aber immer noch gesucht: ein Partner (M

---

120 Brand name of a range of cleaning products.
121 Ross McKibbin (b. 1942) – essayist.
122 See p. 48, n. 41.

bis 50) in den LRB ads. Soviel zur Sucht nach Bestrafung.
Nicht zu erwähnen mein lebenslanges Elend. Na los,
streng dich an. Box no. 0942.[123]

---

123   Translation: 'Though she was a successful investment banker, she was
dissatisfied with her life. Something was missing. She attempted to confront
the many thoughts, moods, and long-held myths that act as barriers to
happiness in personal lives and relationships. Success was defined as making
money, finding the perfect husband, getting to the top in business. And yet,
she pondered, who is genuinely happy? All the people who have achieved these
things – are they really happy? Very probably, she concluded, yet still sought a
partner (M to 50) through the LRB personal ads. Talk about being a glutton for
punishment. Not to mention abject failure and life-long misery. Go on, take
your best shot. Box no. 0942'.

“A 1:128 working scale model of the Karakumsky Canal”

In April 1982, a golfer[124] at the City Park West Municipal Golf Course in New Orleans was killed after he threw his golf club against a golf cart in frustration. The club snapped and the bottom half of the club rebounded and stabbed him in the throat. This wasn't the thing that killed the golfer, however. He was killed when he pulled the club head from his neck, thereby increasing the blood flow and loss from his jugular vein. This, and many more golfing tales, from unemployed after-dinner speaker and part-time pastry chef (M, 58). Box no. 9651.

I composed this advert on the anniversary of the first performance of *Das Rheingold* for a very good reason.[125] Man, 59. Box no. 7011.

My lunch is my life. Amateur griddle chef (M, 51). Box no. 5689.

3 June, 1844. 12 December, 1878. 1 December, 1900. 28 December, 1907. 1 September, 1914. 21 February, 1918. 26 September, 1955. 18 June, 1987. 3 June, 1957. All days on which various species of bird became extinct.[126] Apart from the last one – that's my birthday! Man. Box no. 9611.

---

124 The victim is believed to be 26-year-old Michael Scaglione.

125 *Das Rheingold* – the first of four operas that comprise *Der Ring des Nibelungen* by Richard Wagner. Its first performance was at the National Theatre in Munich on 22 September 1869.

126 3 June, 1844 – great auk (*Pinguinus impennis*); 12 December 1878 – Labrador duck (*Camptorhynchus labradorius*); 1 December 1900 – Guadalupe caracara (*Polyborus lutosus*); 28 December 1907 – huia (*Heteralocha acutirostris*); 1 September 1914 – passenger pigeon (*Ectopistes migratorius*); 21 February 1918 – Carolina parakeet (*Conuropsis carolinensis*); 26 September 1955 – Grenadan Euler's flycatcher (*Lathrotriccus euleri flaviventris*); 18 June 1987 – kaua'i 'Ō'ō (*Moho braccatus*).

There is only one recorded instance of an elephant being sentenced to death by hanging. It was Mary, a circus elephant, in Erwin, Tennessee, September 1916.[127] At the first attempt, the chain placed around her neck snapped under the poor beast's great weight, but the second try was all too successful. Woman, currently researching animal public executions, seeks man to 40 for nights of gentle sobbing and repeating the words 'why, God, why?' while shaking clenched fists at the ceiling. Must have own car. Box no. 6900.

6.10am, January 19, 1977. Snow falls for the first time on West Palm Beach. The snow spreads to Fort Lauderdale by 8.30am, continuing south to Miami and Homestead. At Crandon Park Zoo, heat lamps are brought in to protect the iguanas. True story. Man (35) incapable of making any point whatsoever would like to meet woman to 40 for nights of awkward smiles and sentences that peter off in the middle. Box no. 5991.

In February next year I will begin work in my garden on a 1:128 working scale model of the Karakumsky Canal, which stretches 1,200km from Haun-Khan to Ashkhabad, Turkmenistan. It irrigates a course of 800km and is the largest in the world. Now make love to me. Man, 53. Kettering.[128] Box no. 5889.

Marry me and I will grant you access to the finest collection of mounted albino tiger barbs this side of Gloucester. Osteopath and weekend taxidermist (M, 43). Box no. 4801.

---

127 'Five-ton Mary', as she was known, had stepped on an inexperienced keeper's head while chasing after a watermelon.

128 Kettering – a town in Northamptonshire, situated on the River Ise. It is twinned with Lahnstein in Germany and with Kettering, Ohio.

I hope you're sitting down while reading because this advert might just excite your socks off! Man, 37. Box no. 7695.

The only thing missing in this column is an amphibious car expert who specialises in insurance and reinsurance consultancy. Man, 45. Amphibious car expert specialising in insurance and reinsurance consultancy. Box no. 6011.

A friend once bought me a pair of novelty underpants that had a caption on the front reading 'In case of fire break glass'. I didn't understand what it meant until they did actually catch fire in the tumble dryer because they were acrylic and I had the setting on too high. The door melted shut and sure enough I had to break the glass to put the fire out. Replacement dryers are very expensive. As such I would like to meet a nice woman who won't set fire to my underpants. Stupid, stupid man, 51. Box no. 8050.

I'd like to dedicate this advert to Phil Fondacaro.[129] Box no. 4222.

When Diana Rigg was in *The Avengers* I liked it.[130] But when Diana Rigg wasn't in *The Avengers* I didn't like it. I like Diana Rigg. Are you Diana Rigg? Please write. Box no. 4377.

---

129   Phil Fondacaro (b. 1958) – American actor. Measuring three feet, six inches tall, Fondacaro played the only ewok to have a death scene in *Star Wars: Episode VI – Return of the Jedi* (1983, dir. Richard Marquand) and the shortest ever on-screen Dracula in Charles Band's *The Creeps* (1997).

130   *The Avengers* – television series about secret-agent operatives, broadcast on the ITV network and running from 1961 to 1969. Diana Rigg (b. 1938) played Emma Peel in the series from 1965 to 1967.

I am the only valid reason to visit St Albans.
Ambidextrous psychiatrist and amateur fire-eater (F, 37).[131]
Box no. 5483.

Nepenthes rajah.[132] It's an insectivorous pitcher plant
species with an urn-shaped trap so large it has been
observed digesting rats and other mammalian species.
I find it a continual source of inspiration and the single
most impressive organism on the planet. Woman, 34,
WLTM man to 40. Kent. Box no. 5993.

---

131   St Albans also has a cathedral and a fifteenth-century clock tower.

132   Member of the monotypic *Nepenthaceae* family. Endemic to Mount
Kinabalu and neighbouring Mount Tambuyukon in Sabah, Malaysian Borneo.

"A time capsule of despair"

Man, 41. Will you marry me? Anybody? Box no. 8976.

They say the pram in the hallway is the enemy of art. Not true. Astaroth, Threshold Guardian of the Infernal Plane[133] is the enemy of art. Join me in my battle to rid this world of his Satanic intent by sending care-home vouchers to his long-suffering daughter and one-time sculpturing genius, 37, box no. 9361.

When I inevitably read this ad again in a 'laugh-out loud' follow-up volume of 'hilarious', 'quirky' and 'endearing' lonely hearts ads, it will be like opening a time capsule of despair on the emptiest period of my pathetic existence. Unless you write now and agree to marry me. No pressure from 'winning', 'charming', 'best loo-read' F, 38.[134] Box no. 8563.

Herring-bone Artex.[135] It could be yours. But you'd also have to take gorgeous, nubile, 30-year old Eng Lit post-grad. Also woodchip wallpaper from 1972 and a grandmother who refuses to go into care. Box no. 9730.

LRB readers! You are all invited to my wedding. One lucky guest will also be picked to be my groom. Dress is smart/casual and hymn sheets will be provided by desperate, clutching F (41 and not getting any younger, or thinner, or more fertile) at box no. 2457.

---

133 The Prince of Hell, according to demonologists.

134 See p. 25, n. 15, and p. 53, n. 43.

135 Artex – a surface coating trademarked and manufactured by Artex, Ltd. Artex is used on ceilings where it can be textured to carry pattens (such as herring-bone, which was popular in the early eighties).

Short-changed by the pie-vendor of love. Hamstrung on the pitch of reason. Man, 34, stuck in the lower divisions of passion, where the players are always part-time, and the action (blundered, chaotic and often resulting in injury) is only every second Sunday. Urgently needs woman with good shin-pads, half-time oranges and experience of serial playoff disappointment. Must be embittered by years of following Dagenham & Redbridge.[136] No seats on my terrace at box no. 1012.

Agerum, Alvine, Lång, Delikat, Drälla, Fågelbo, Igge, Ordning, Utgård. Gentleman to 50 familiar with the simple poetry of Ikea, and no stranger to flat-pack assembly, urgently sought by woman currently living in a tee-pee in her own living room. Putting together my Noresund is no guarantee of sex but it does put you a long way up the waiting list. Box no. 9073.

Coffee. Coffee. Coffee. Coffee. Malteser! Be the sweetie worth ploughing my way through love's harshest Revel's bag for.[137] Man, 36. Box no. 8361.

---

136 Dagenham & Redbridge Football Club – Association Football club, founded in 1992 after a merger between Dagenham and Redbridge Forest.

137 Revels – spherical chocolate confection with assorted fillings. Because the fillings are mostly indistinguishable from each other (apart from the Galaxy Counters, which are flat), it is difficult to correctly guess the flavour of each one pulled from the pack – the single most disappointing Revel being coffee, whilst the Malteser (a malt honeycomb centre) is the prized possession. Because Maltesers are available as a confection in their own right, with their own branding, it is assumed that one of the principal pleasures of Revels is the 'Russian Roulette' element of risk at drawing unpopular flavours.

Wanted: rich, deaf and blind woman to take my irascible old fart of a father off my hands. Must like the *Telegraph*. Box no. 9470.

Beard. Have one? Want one? Box no. 1315.

This column is not a great place for meeting like-minded people. It is the Third Bolgia of the Eighth Circle of Hell for lonely literary types. Woman, 46, finally ready to stare defeat in the face after three ads and 41 responses from goblin perverts.[138] Box no. 2220.

Your Christmas bookings now taken! Pathetic man, 37. Box no. 9641.

myspace.com/mantellinghimselfheisnotyetoverthehill whenreallyheis or box no. 8743.

Stare at the back of your hand for 30 seconds. Now stare at this advert for 15 seconds whilst squinting your eyes. Now fully open your eyes and stare at the back of your hand for another 30 seconds. Advert. And again at your hand. Now stare at your mother. Back of your hand. Advert. Hand. Advert. Mother. Mother. Hand. Mother. Wall. Feet. Now wipe the tears away. Back at the hand. Advert. Hand. Mother. Man, 43. Hand. Advert. Mother. Hand. Hand. Hand. Box no. 8936. Mother.

138 A reference to Dante's *Divine Comedy*. The poem, written in first person, tells of Dante's journey through the three realms of the dead: *Inferno*, *Purgatorio*, and *Paradiso*. The Eighth Circle of Hell is described in *Inferno* and is reserved for those committing sins of fraud or treachery. It is divided into ten concentric circular ditches or bolgie (the Eighth Circle is called the Malebolge, literally 'evil ditches'). The Third Bolgia, mentioned in the advert, houses those guilty of the sin of simony (the ecclesiastical crime of paying for offices or positions within a church hierarchy, named after Simon Magus, who appears in the Acts of the Apostles 8:18–24).

Word to yo moms – I came to drop bombs. I got more rhymes than the bible's got psalms.[139] Classics lecturer (M, 62). To some I'm possibly the single most embarrassing person at any social gathering. To others I'm fly-er than the zipper on yo pants. 4reals. Laters. Or something. Please make love to me. Box no. 9749.

1996 was the best year of my life. 2003 wasn't too bad either. If you can figure out a pattern I'll marry you. Dentist and evening Lars Ulrich[140] fantasist. 54. Male. Box no. 9709.

I met all my previous lovers at Costco (I only needed one, but came away with thirty). That changes right here, right now, with a call to all men to 45 allergic to generic vodka brands and bulk purchase pastries. It's cash only, and you must show your membership card upon entry (parking strictly limited to two hours, one trolley per customer during peak hours). Box no. 1553.

---

139 Taken from 'Jump Around' – written by Everlast and performed by House of Pain. Taken from the album *House of Pain* (1992, XL Recordings). The song reached number three in the US charts, with a remixed version getting to number eight in the UK charts.

140 Lars Ulrich (b. 1963) – drummer with heavy metal band Metallica. Born to a middle-class family in Gentofte, Denmark, Ulrich was a tennis prodigy and moved to Los Angeles, California, when he was seventeen to pursue his tennis training. Ulrich's father, Torben Ulrich, was an acclaimed tennis professional during the late 1970s and early 1980s. In 1976 he was the world's top-ranked tennis player. Lars Ulrich became a vocal opponent of Internet-based file-sharing programs such as Napster, and, with the rest of Metallica, sued the company in April 2000 for copyright infringement.

"Hubris made me pen this ad"

If partaking of the grape too eagerly after a messy break-up has taught me anything, it's that answer-phone messages are admissible in divorce courts as evidence of 'unreasonable behaviour'. But if you're a 35–45 year old guy who knows when a lady needs space and is able to take threats of physical assault and arson in the humorous, ironically edgy way in which they're intended, then write to beautiful, vivacious, newly-medicated F, 38. Box no. 0784.

My winning streak in this column is about to come to an abrupt halt with the placing of this ad. Man. 38. Box no. 3499.

Ordinarily I shun all things pertaining to the nefarious world of dating – personal ads, matchmaking agencies, over-zealous friends who 'know someone perfect'. But right now I'm unemployed, alcoholic, medicated and haven't had my bones jumped for a year. Hit me up. Woman, 37. Box no. 7799.

Hubris made me pen this ad. You will answer, of course, but only ironically. Man, once great and 23, now alone and 51. Box no. 0420.

Serial personal advertiser (Man, 33) – ninth time lucky? Probably not. Here's to another £14.80. Box no. 5029.

Less *Chicken Soup for the Soul*,[141] more *Lobster Bisque for the Glutes* – rejected self-help-manual author and fitness instructor (M, 38) seeks in-shape F to 40 for

141 *Chicken Soup for the Soul* – series of motivational books written by Jack Canfield and Mark Victor Hansen and published by Vermilion.

evenings constructing publishable titbits on overcoming depression, enhancing the strength of a weakened pelvic floor,[142] and questionable shell-fish aphrodisia. Must enjoy light bondage. Box no. 8721.

IT savant (M, 37) unexceptional in most things but blessed with uncanny ability to remember every wrong ever done to him and to bring them all up on the very rare occasions he's invited to the pub after work. WLTM woman to 40 who preferably doesn't speak English, is very bad at interpreting facial gestures and to whom a clenched fist snapping pens in half doesn't mean a promotion at work has once again passed me by and gone to the least qualified member of staff but is a sign of glorious victory in the power struggle against my tyrannous employers and their idiot ways. Viva La Revolución! Then pass me my beta-blockers at Box no. 0889.

When life gives you lemons, don't make lemonade – instead squeeze it into the face of your cheating arse of a husband then cut the legs off every pair of trousers he owns. Sensitive F, 45. Ready to move on and begin her life a-fresh with man willing to provide time-sheets and supporting documentary evidence for every minute of his time out of the house. Box no. 9078.

This personal ad is the product of an entire evening spent eating acid.[143] Man, 63. Box no. 1211.

Safety first. Dignity second. Trousers last. Rubbish wok-cooked foods enthusiast and flammable materials-wearing

---

142 See p.71, n. 65.

143 Lysergic acid diethylamide, LSD, or acid – a semi-synthetic psychedelic drug.

loon (M) WLTM F to 45 with fire-blanket and no small amount of knowledge regarding the correct batter-frying procedures of tempura.[144] Bicester. Box no. 3299.

....

My life is an endless hell of *Little Britain* quotes, rugby shirts worn with the collars turned up in a non-ironic way, England flags attached to every car window, holidays to Whitby, two-minute sex, golf anecdotes, boxed wine, bumping into 'Bob from the office' in the frozen food aisle at Safeway as he fills his trolley with bulk purchases of Findus Crispy Pancakes, self-assembly bookcases staying in their cardboard boxes in the corner of the kitchen for six months, disposable tongue scrapers, did I say two-minute sex, the 'art house film' he had in mind being *The Da Vinci Code*, discount CDs called 'Dance Anthems Vol. 13' bought from gas stations, punctuated only by self-loathing and impotent dreams of revenge that I wish I had the energy to manifest into reality. Woman, 34, seeks man/divorce lawyer/assassin to explore possibilities, payment plans, poetry.[145] Box no. 1198.

....

144 A constant temperature is thought to be crucial to making tempura. As such, ice is often added to the batter mixture to prevent fried tempura soaking up too much oil during the frying process. Also, tempura should be fried in small batches to ensure an even distribution of heat throughout each. After each batch has been fried, pieces of loose batter should be removed from the frying oil, otherwise they will alter the heat distribution. Over-mixing tempura batter results in the production of gluten, which makes the fried batter too chewy.

145 *Little Britain* – character-based sketch show serialized first on BBC radio and then television. Written by and starring Matt Lucas (b. 1974) and David Walliams (b. 1971). Findus Crispy Pancakes – crepes coated with breadcrumbs. Sold in the UK and Sweden. They are available frozen in packs of four with one of three fillings: cheese, minced beef and chicken, bacon and sweet corn. *The Da Vinci Code* – Columbia Pictures adaptation of the Dan Brown novel of the same name. The book was published in 2003, and the film (dir. Ron Howard) released in 2006.

Fear. Alienation. Irrational hatred. Compulsive teeth-brushing. If only I'd read the reverse of my ex-wife's business card before jumping into bed with her and signing away a decade of happiness and my house in Surrey. You can write if you like, but I'm going to have to ask for the phone numbers of at least two past employers and five previous lovers. Box no. 8908.

'Scarface', 'Mad Dog', 'Pretty Boy', 'Baby Face' – if I had an underworld crime nickname it would be 'Screwed by Ex-Wife's Solicitor and Currently Sleeping in a Caravan'.[146] Man, 42. Screwed by ex-wife's solicitor and currently sleeping in a caravan. Box no. 5543.

The complete list of my sexual conquests: 1994–95 – Anna; 1996 – Julia, Alison; 1997 – Italian girl at Karl's party, Claire (Clare?), Jessica (fingered); 1998 – Anna again (big mistake), receptionist at my second temp job (possibly called Helena), Becky (I was in love but she went back to her boyfriend); 1999 – Jeremy's girlfriend; 2000–01 – Karolina (deported); 2002 – woman at nightclub, woman at nightclub, woman at nightclub, woman at Stewart's barbecue, Stewart (accidental coming together of groins, the three of us were naked and very, very drunk), woman at nightclub; 2003–06 – Evil Satanic Bitch Whore; 2007 – the Internet. LRB-reading women to 35 – don't pretend your relationships have been any less incongruous and unsatisfying. Write to probably the most normal guy you'll ever see in a lonely heart advert and maybe we'll end up friends or lovers or despising each other and wincing every time we remember our awful one-night stand or maybe

---

146 Nicknames given to infamous gangsters: 'Scarface' – Al Capone (1899–1947); 'Mad Dog' – Vincent Coll (born Uinseann Ó Colla, 1908–32); 'Pretty Boy' – Charles Floyd (1904–34); 'Baby Face' – Lester Joseph Gillis (1908–34).

we'll get married or have children. Writing's a good start though. Man, 31. Box no. 3243.

If it wasn't for this column I'd be the loneliest man alive. Box no. 4335.

Week 3 – Day 2. Breakfast: small piece of fruit (for example an apple), two crispbreads with one tablespoon low-fat soft cheese and one sliced tomato. Lunch: one wholemeal pita bread with a quarter small pot reduced-fat hummus and crudités, one small banana. Dinner: 47 chocolate cakes, anguish, despair, bile, hatred, a small pot of low-fat fruit yoghurt. Post-divorce comfort eater and sex therapist (F, 38). Box no. 9977.

Get out. And don't come back. If these are the words that greet you upon waking every morning, why not join me – man, 51, completely incapable of realising when he's outstayed his welcome. Clinging on like shit to a shovel at box no. 8017.

'Your feelings towards your partner may change for the worse on Wednesday when they act in what you perceive to be an inappropriate way in the cold meats section of Waitrose by ordering a sliced Italian ham that you specifically didn't want for a small evening meal you're thinking of preparing for some mutual friends. Console yourself by leaving him immediately, burning all his underwear and writing to his parents to tell them he's secretly gay'. My (now ex) girlfriend's astrological reading for March 22 this year was uncannily accurate. Man, 34, WLTM woman who isn't a Virgo Rooster.[147] Box no. 6678.

147 Virgo – 23 August to 22 September in the tropical zodiac, or 16 September to 15 October (approximately) in the sidereal zodiac. Rooster – in the Chinese zodiac, 22 January 1909–9 February 1910, 8 February 1921–27 January 1922,

This ad has appeared before. Last time, though, it was funnier. And better looking. And didn't have to worry about CSA[148] payments. Box no. 4322.

Just once I'd like to date a woman whose home isn't on Bitch Island, accessible only by the Train of the Damned[149] into which is continuously piped the blood-curdling screams of her multitudinous previous victims. If you don't think that's too much to ask – and don't have a long-running tab at your local pharmacist – then write to stupid man, 43. Box no. 6544.

The last time I wrote a lonely heart advert my dog ate it and subsequently choked to death. I'm hoping for better results with this one. Woman. 38. Box no. 5435.

My resolution for 2007 was to finish my PhD, go running every day, reduce my intake of toxins, give up smoking, travel across India and the Far East, fix the hinge on the refrigerator door and make peace with my estranged father. I achieved only one of these. This year my resolution is to remember to put my trousers on every day. Man, 43. The fridge opens like a dream at box no. 5427.

'Du bist eine Maultasche'. Not, it transpires, the correct greeting when welcoming an 'art' publisher. Gullible

---

26 January 1933–13 February 1934, 13 February 1945–1 February 1946, 31 January 1957–17 February 1958, 17 February 1969–5 February 1970, 5 February 1981–24 January 1982, 23 January 1993–9 February 1994, 9 February 2005–28 January 2006.

148   CSA: Child Support Agency. Responsible for the calculation, collection and distribution of child-maintenance payments from non-resident to resident parents.

149   Possibly the Virgin Trains West Coast Main Line between Liverpool Lime Street and London Euston, which is shit.

publicity exec (F, 28) and the butt of all the jokes with the Frankfurt 'in-crowd' seeks avuncular M to 40 with penchant for hitting enemies with sticks.[150] Box no. 5400.

The Red Devils flew over this ad while I was writing it.[151] Family fun day guy (divorced, 51); monster trucks, motorbike displays, St John's Ambulance and a beer tent. That's me, breaking my leg on the Marine Corps death slide of self-hatred and over-compensation at box no. 8769. I'll meet you by the face-painting stand.

MISTEAK! Spt the deliberit errers in this ad and ern £££'s working from home or as an editer on wan of are countrys leeding jurnels. Or else let's meet for coffee and whine about the state of modern publishing for a good three hours whilst slowly getting drunk before going back to your place (my flatmate is 72 and makes pig noises in his sleep) and having clumsy, immediately regrettable sex. Man, 35. Still bitter over poor career decisions made a decade ago. Hoxton. Box no. 8900.

Mid-twenties, divorced, ex-secondary school teacher. Likes the lights out, the curtains closed, Simon and Garfunkel singing 'Scarborough Fair',[152] and quiet reminiscences about mother's herb garden. Would like to

---

150 'Du bist eine Maultasche' translates as 'You are my ravioli'. The advertiser is referring to the Frankfurt Book Fair, or Frankfurter Buchmesse, the world's largest trade fair for the publishing industry.

151 Red Devils – the Parachute Regiment's display team. Formed on 1 January 1964 by Lt.-Col. Glyn Gilbert, then Regimental Colonel of the Parachute Regiment, it was officially declared the British Army's parachute display team in 1979. A popular attraction at provincial fetes and summer fairs where they often display their skills.

152 'Scarborough Fair/Canticle' – traditional English ballad, recorded by Simon and Garfunkel on their album *Parsley, Sage, Rosemary and Thyme* (1966, Columbia Records).

hear from sympathetic Christians with recipes using rock salt and dill. Box no. 7989.

Who knows what tomorrow will bring? Amateur roadkill/wild mushroom chef living the Hugh Fearnley-Whittingstall dream (F, 34) is fairly certain it will be a stray cat and another night of unwanted psychedelic flashes. Thanks for nothing River Cottage. Also the A405.[153] Box no. 8979.

Prevent your new-cut sweeping fringe from parting in the centre by blow-drying in the opposite direction to the way you want it to go using a flat brush. The natural parting will be gone, as will your boyfriend who perversely resents your hairstyling tips, but it will keep the hair laying flat with a nice sweep. Man, 46. Camp as custard. Box no. 0770.

This town isn't big enough for the both of us. Failed urban planner. M, 48. Didsbury.[154] Box no. 9876.

---

153 Hugh Fearnley-Whittingstall (b. 1965) – celebrity chef and presenter of the *River Cottage* series of cookery programmes, along with *A Cook on the Wild Side*, in which he ate roadkill animals, and *TV Dinners*, in which he cooked and ate a human placenta served as a pâté. The A405 is the North Orbital Trunk Road (M25 Junction 21A to M10/A414 Park Street Roundabout) and is located in St Albans (see p. 126, n. 131).

154 Population 14,292 (Census 2001). The population density at the time of the 2001 census was 5,276/square mile (2,037/km²), which is significantly lower than the Manchester area, 9,880.8/square mile (3,815/km²), of which Didsbury is a suburb. However, the area is intersected by Wilmslow Road, which, according to analysts, is the busiest bus corridor in Europe.

"You know who
you are"

All too often the companion adjective to those used by men in this column ('intelligent', 'witty', 'creative', 'funny', etc.) is 'psychopath'.[155] Being remembered as the blind date who stabbed himself in the back of the hand if I carried out my threat to leave the restaurant unless the crying stopped is not a good thing. You know who you are. Woman. 40. No nutters. Box no. 6343.

This isn't a lonely heart column. It is an occult ritual that opens a gateway to hell itself. Such is my conclusion after my only previous respondent turned out to be the Devil's Hell Bitch with a sulphurous heart and talons for fingers. You know who you are. Subscribe not to the temptations held within. Although if you're not the Devil's Hell Bitch and enjoy classical music, contemporary art and theatre, why not write to finance consultant, M, 46. Whitstable. Box no. 3400.

'Good news! My favourite flavour of crisp is in production again!' If this is a sentiment you have ever expressed or conceived in adulthood, you needn't write. You know who you are. F, 32. Box no. 9091.

I suppose the end began with me paying for the meal and all the drinks. The brief relationship was practically over by the time he told me that he hadn't brought cash with him and could I pay for the taxi? The formal departure, however, came with his attempt to push his debit card into my mouth and tap out his pin number on my forehead after I'd asked 'do you think I'm an ATM?' (You know who you are). LRB-

---

155 Statistically, the most commonly used companion adjective for male advertisers in the LRB personals column is 'divorced'.

reading men – either you have small change always about your person or it's a long walk home back from beautiful and, until last Friday week, reasonably indifferent towards even the most stupid of men F (London, 43). Box no. 5431.

Is there a charming man out there – warm, spontaneous, knowing? If so, could you reply to all the men currently appearing in this column and give them a few pointers? Attractive, educated woman, 46, fed up of having to fake emergency phone calls to avoid pre-dessert ramblings about your sister's new conservatory and how much respect you have for Enya.[156] You know who you are. Box no. 9980.

Placing this advert does not mean I have suddenly become a pervert shepherd. You know who you are. Photos of you clothed and without your collection of porcelain Napoleonic soldiers, please, or not at all to impatient woman, 34, sitting firmly atop of a hillock of normalcy. Box no. 4444.

Don't refer to your biceps as 'guns' and you may stand a chance of me not wanting to kill you at the next LRB singles night. You know who you are. F, 37. Always remembers a face and any subsequent associations of despair. Box no. 8791.

To the guy with the wild grey hair and thin pony tail and bow-tie and white socks and chewed copy of Rimbaud[157] and the lisp and excessive spittle and over-use of the word 'platitudes' and faint odour of taco meat who will no

---

156   Enya (born Eithne Patricia Ní Bhraonáin, 1961) – Irish singer, songwriter, and former member of Clannad (she left the band in 1982).

157   Jean Nicolas Arthur Rimbaud (1854–91). French poet.

doubt reply to this advert much like he's replied to every other advert I've ever placed in here: 'eccentric' is only a favourable adjective when it's wrapped in an attractive package or earns over £200,000 a year and owns a holiday retreat in Tuscany. Other LRB-reading men should also note this. Replies from 'normals' or the stupidly rich only please to woman, 45, currently down to 37 seconds on her 'tolerance of idiots' meter. Box no. 4722.

No. You cannot show me your interpretation of what our love-making might look like if animated by Ray Harryhausen in an early Sinbad film.[158] You know who you are. F, 39. Croydon. Box no. 4811.

'Lait. Oh Dieu!' Woman, 51, seeks LRB reading man to 55 whose social skills and language acquisition are somewhat in advance of those of the Wild Boy of Aveyron (you know who you are).[159] Box no. 7901.

My last affair ended with a round of applause from a crew of stand-by paramedics. If the next one has to end I'll settle

158 Raymond Frederick Harryhausen (b. 1920) – American film producer and special effects creator. Known for his brand of stop-motion model animation. *The 7th Voyage of Sinbad* (1958, dir. Nathan H. Juran) is the first of the Harryhausen-conceptualized and animated Sinbad trilogy (the others being *The Golden Voyage of Sinbad*, released in 1974, and *Sinbad and the Eye of the Tiger*, 1977).

159 Victor of Aveyron, aka the Wild Boy of Aveyron, was found wandering the woods near Saint-Sernin-sur-Rance, France (near Toulouse) in 1797. After being captured and escaping several times, he finally emerged from the forests voluntarily on 8 January 1800. Victor was taken under the wing of French physician Jean Marc Gaspard Itard (1774–1838). Itard believed that the two crucial differences between humans and animals were empathy and language and attempted to teach Victor to speak and show human emotion. However, the only words that Victor learned to speak were 'lait' (milk) and 'Oh Dieu' (oh God). It is now thought, partly by studying such feral children, that language acquisition takes place in a critical period of early childhood.

for a text message. Woman, 39. Seeks man who knows when to wear his Medic Alert Badge, carries his own emergency injectable adrenaline kit, and isn't too scared to say 'actually, I don't feel like lobster tonight'. You know who you are. Box no. 7942.

Woman, 36, WLTM man to 40 who doesn't try to high-five her after sex. You know who you are. Box no. 7438.

Woman, 38. WLTM man to 45 who doesn't name his genitals after German chancellors. You know who you are and, no, I don't want to meet either Bismarck, Bethmann-Hollweg, or Prince Chlodwig zu Hohenlohe-Schillingsfürst, however admirable the independence he gave to secretaries of state may have been.[160] Box no. 5739.

160 Otto Eduard Leopold von Bismarck (1815–98) – Prussian and German statesman of the nineteenth century. As Minister-President of Prussia from 1862 to 1890, he oversaw the unification of Germany. Theobald von Bethmann-Hollweg (1856–1921) – Chancellor of the German Empire from 1909 to 1917. Prince Chlodwig zu Hohenlohe-Schillingsfürst, Chlodwig Carl Viktor, Fürst zu Hohenlohe-Schillingsfürst, Fürst von Ratibor und Corvey (1819–1901) – Chancellor of Germany from 1894 to 1900. It was, in fact, the Prince of Hohenlohe-Schillingsfürst's advanced years during his tenure as Chancellor and subsequently increasingly rare appearances at Prussian and German parliaments (he was seventy-five when he accepted the office at the request of Kaiser Wilhelm II) that led to increased independence being granted to the German secretaries of state.

Appendix
A chronology of Miss World title holders, 1951–2008

1951 Kerstin Håkansson, Sweden.
Originally called the Festival Bikini Contest and part of the 1951 Festival of Britain, the beauty pageant created by Eric Morley (Public Relations Officer of festival organizers Mecca, Ltd.) attracted so much publicity that it soon became known as 'Miss World' by the international press, prompting Morley to trademark the title. Håkansson would, in fact, be the only winner in a bikini as future competitions switched to the one-piece bathing suit. Morley said some years later that Håkansson 'filled a bikini more perfectly than anyone I have seen, before or since, and among all the Miss World winners she ranks as just about the most delectable'. She received a cheque for £1,000 and a pearl necklace.

1952 May Louise Flodin, Sweden.
Belgian entry Anne-Marie Pauwels was disqualified after refusing to be separated from her boyfriend during the contest.

1953 Denise Perrier, France.
Runner-up Marina Papaelia (Egypt) collapsed screaming as Perrier was proclaimed Miss World. She recovered, continuing to participate in subsequent news interviews and photo sessions, although, when asked by a news reporter to comment on the winner, she remarked, 'I think she stink!' Perrier, who was a convent schoolgirl prior to the contest, appeared in an uncredited role in the 1971 James Bond film *Diamonds Are Forever*, where she was strangled with her own swimsuit by Sean Connery before revealing the location of Ernst Stavro Blofeld.

1954 Antigone Costanda, Egypt.

1955 Susana Duijm, Venezuela.

1956 Petra Schürmann, West Germany.

1957 Marita Lindahl, Finland.

1958 Penelope Coelen, South Africa.

'It's just wonderful. Just think – I was only Miss South Africa yesterday.' Penelope Coelen speaking on the telephone to reporters after winning.

1959 Corine Rottschafer, Holland.

Non-finalist Miss United States Loretta Powell accused Rottschafer of 'padding her bra'. Rottschafer disproved this after changing into a one-piece swimsuit for the measuring ceremony, which confirmed her 37-22-37 statistics. Miss Bermuda was found to be an impostor and was disqualified.

1960 Norma Cappagli, Argentina.

Cappagli was threatened with disqualification after revealing that she liked to unwind at the end of a long day of rehearsing by drinking a glass or two of Scotch. She defended herself by asking 'Where does it say in the rules that I can be disqualified for having a late-night drink if I want one?' Fourth runner-up Judith Ann Achter (Miss United States) only came second in her national event, but was flown to London two days after the original entry, Annette Driggers, had been disqualified for being underage.

1961 Rosemarie Frankland, United Kingdom.

Frankland suffered depression and panic syndrome throughout her life and died in December 2000. It was never confirmed whether her death was a result of suicide or an accidental prescription-drug overdose, although she had told a newspaper not long beforehand that 'beauty queens are dressed up and paraded down the catwalk just so some fellow can get a quick thrill. They should shove it [Miss World] in the archives and forget about it'.

1962 Catharina Lodders, Netherlands.

'I don't think I'm the most beautiful girl in the world. . . . I am the most beautiful girl here.' Catharina Johanna Lodders to reporters after winning.

1963 Carole Crawford, Jamaica.

1964 Ann Sydney, United Kingdom.

1965 Lesley Langley, United Kingdom.

Langley was almost dethroned after nude photos of her surfaced during her tenure as Miss World. However, because they were taken before her entry into the pageant, she was allowed to keep her title. The same controversy and conclusion would appear again in 1969 during the reign of Eva Rueber-Staier.

1966 Reita Faria, India.

Uzor Okafor of Nigeria was disqualified because there had been no Miss Nigeria contest. The Nigerian Deputy High Commissioner in London stated 'our government does not sponsor beauty contestants'. Paquita Torres Pérez of Spain withdrew from the contest because of the presence of Miss Gibraltar. She told newspapers 'as an Andalusian the British flag over the Rock offends me'. Meanwhile Priscilla Martenstyn admitted, 'I am not the real Miss Ceylon. I am a schoolgirl in London.' The real Miss Ceylon – Lorraine Roosmalecocq – was in the USA for the rival Miss Universe pageant.

1967 Madeleine Hartog Bell, Peru.

1968 Penelope Plummer, Australia.

Miss Philippines, Cecilia Amabuyok, was a novice Roman Catholic nun. At a banquet given before the Miss World contest by Britain's Variety Club, the men wolf-whistled, stamped their feet, and hoisted her onto a table. She finished in fourth place. Spain's Maria Amparo Rodrigo Lorenza walked out the night before the finals when Miss Gibraltar refused to apologize for saying that she was glad Miss Spain was in the contest. Spain had declined to participate in Miss World for several years due to the presence of Miss Gibraltar. On the same evening as Miss Spain's withdrawal, Lebanon's Lili Bissar was disqualified after it was discovered she was only fifteen years old.

1969 Eva Rueber-Staier, Austria.

See 1965.

1970 Jennifer Hosten, Grenada.

The 1970 contest began with a row over South Africa being allowed to enter two contestants; one white (Miss South Africa), and one black (Miss Africa South). In the evening of the event itself, Women's Liberation activists protested and threw flour at the host, Bob Hope. He was heckled after making sexist jokes on stage ('It's been quite a cattle market – I've been back there checking calves'), then later remarked, 'Anyone who would try and break up an affair as wonderful as this has got to be on some kind of dope.' The protesters were arrested and their subsequent trial was billed as 'The first Women's Lib. trial since the Suffragettes'. Argument also centred on the title being awarded to the Miss Grenada contestant, Hosten, who won having received just two 'first' votes compared to Sweden's nine. The Prime Minister of Grenada, Sir Eric Gairy, was on the judging panel. In 1979, Gairy was overthrown as Prime Minister because of charges of corruption and human-rights abuses.

1971 Lúcia Petterle, Brazil.

1972 Belinda Green, Australia.

1973 Marjorie Wallace, United States.

Sacked as Miss World 104 days after winning the title because, according to the organizers, she had 'failed to fulfil the basic requirements of the job'. Elsewhere it was suggested that the real reason behind her losing the crown was her alleged statement during a public engagement, 'As Miss World I can get laid with any man I pick.'

1974 Helen Morgan, United Kingdom.

The second Welsh woman and fourth UK candidate to win Miss World lost her title within four days of being crowned after it was discovered she was an unmarried mother. Although this didn't break the rules of the contest (which stipulated only that contestants must be unmarried) she was forced to resign. Miss Venezuela, Alicia Rivas, said, 'In my country, a girl who has a baby without being married is regarded as a bad girl, not pure and undefiled as we are led to believe Miss World should be.'

1974 Anneline Kriel, South Africa (replacing Helen Morgan).

1975 Wilnelia Merced, Puerto Rico.

During an unscreened preliminary round in the swimsuit event, four of the French-speaking competitors (from Belgium, France, Luxembourg, and Mauritius) refused to turn to be judged from behind, with Mariella Tse-Sik-Sun (Miss Mauritius) later stating, 'It is degrading for a girl to have to show her bottom to the judges. We refused to be treated like slave girls.'

1976 Cindy Breakspeare, Jamaica.

Seeing the continued indulgence of South Africa to enter a white and a black contestant (under the titles Miss South Africa and Miss Africa South respectively) as a tacit endorsement of apartheid, nine contestants withdrew (India, Mauritius, Liberia, Malaysia, Philippines, Seychelles, Sri Lanka, Swaziland, and Yugoslavia).

1977 Mary Stävin, Sweden.

Miss Italy, Anna Kanakis, and Miss Malta, Janice Galea, were both disqualified for being only fifteen. 'They never told me anything about it in Italy,' protested Kanakis. 'I didn't know you had to be seventeen.' The protests against the presence of Miss South Africa continued, leading to South Africa being banned from competing until the end of apartheid in 1991.

1978 Silvana Rosa Suárez, Argentina.

Miss Tunisia, Malek Nemlaghi, was disqualified for refusing

to take off her traditional Muslim veil and pose in a T-shirt and shorts. She eventually changed her mind and was reinstated.

1979 Gina Ann Swainson, Bermuda.

Miss Venezuela, Tatiana Capote, was disqualified after one of her breasts became exposed during a preview of the swimsuit round.

1980 Gabriella Brum, West Germany.

Brum resigned within a day of winning the title. Her boyfriend, pornographic film-maker Benno Bellenbaum, was accused by pageant organizer Julia Morley of 'enticing Gabriella to give up her title'. Bellenbaum, describing himself in interviews at the time as being a 'very young fifty-two', told reporters, 'I won't deny that I would be relieved in many ways if she isn't Miss World.' He added, 'She wants to come home . . . our love is so strong and so young and we want to be together. Her home is here with me. We just love being together, staying in, cooking and reading.' Brum (who was eighteen at the time) meanwhile described the other contestants as 'a bunch of bitches'. When it was suggested that she had posed nude for magazines, Bellenbaum explained, 'She has posed nude only for me, not for anyone else. She's just a fun-loving girl who has never done anything wrong.'

1980 Kimberley Santos, Guam (replacing Gabriella Brum).

1981 Pilín León, Venezuela.

1982 Mariasela Álvarez, Dominican Republic.

Miss Bermuda, Heather Ross, was charged with illegally importing cocaine valued at £200,000 into Britain. She was arrested at Heathrow Airport after stepping off a plane from Amsterdam, nine days after the Miss World contest in which she was unplaced. She served thirteen months of a three-year sentence. Of the winner, Miss Germany, Kerstin Paeserack, remarked, 'They might as well rename the contest Miss Virgin World. All they want is a safe little virgin who will trot around visiting hospitals for them. And that is what they got. It was a farce.' Miss Italy, Raffaella del Rosario, offered, 'There is something strange about her face. Her mouth is too big, and her chin sticks out.'

1983 Sarah-Jane Hutt, United Kingdom.

Miss Jamaica, Catherine Levy, boycotted the coronation ball in protest at being placed fourth. Miss Barbados, Nina McIntosh-Clarke, said of the winner, 'She was not the prettiest girl. We all think the judges were wrong.'

1984 Astrid Carolina Herrera, Venezuela.

1985 Hólmfríður Karlsdóttir, Iceland.

1986 Giselle Laronde, Trinidad and Tobago.

Miss USA, Halle Berry, provoked gasps and complaints from the audience and fellow contestants when she appeared in her national costume – a skimpy flesh-coloured body stocking, embroidered with beads and a few carefully-placed stars. She said that it was supposed to represent 'America's advancement in space', although she later admitted that she wanted to 'catch the eye from the start'. Miss Holland, Janny Tervelde, said, 'We think it's very unfair. I'm totally concealed by wearing the Dutch traditional costume with clogs.'

1987 Ulla Weigerstorfer, Austria.

1988 Linda Pétursdóttir, Iceland.

1989 Aneta Kręglicka, Poland.

The broadcasting rights to the pageant held by Thames Television were not renewed after Thames bowed to pressure from feminist movements. Eric Morley told press, 'They said it was outdated, sexist and not appropriate for modern Britain. I've heard that for the last twenty-five years.'

1990 Gina Tolleson, United States.

1991 Ninibeth Leal, Venezuela.

1992 Julia Kourotchkina, Russia.

1993 Lisa Hanna, Jamaica.

When Israel's Tamara Porat and Lebanon's Ghada Turk were photographed smiling shoulder-to-shoulder, there was political uproar in their respective countries, with Lebanon's top public prosecutor Munif Oueidat stating that he intended to try Miss Lebanon for 'collaborating with the enemy'. Turk argued that she did not realize she was standing next to Miss Israel when the photo was taken. It was four months before she was allowed back to her country, where she immediately faced a military judge on charges of treason.

1994 Aishwarya Rai, India.

1995 Jacqueline Aguilera, Venezuela.

Hours after winning the Miss Personality award, Toyin Enitan Raji, Miss Nigeria, was barred from the contest following worldwide condemnation of the execution of nine dissidents, including Ken Saro-Wiwa, by the Nigerian government of Sani Abacha just days earlier.

1996 Irene Skliva, Greece.

Concerned at the apparent commodification of the female form and the undermining of Indian culture, the contest – held in Bangalore, India – was marred by ongoing violent protests. One man committed suicide by setting himself on fire. Five days before the contest, protesters including activists of the All India Women's Democratic Association (AIDWA) were beaten by the police during a demonstration, with at least four hundred being detained until the evening. Police swung bamboo canes, fired rubber bullets and launched tear gas at the protesters. Members of the Forum for Awakening Women threatened its members would mingle with spectators and immolate themselves after taking poison. The protesters argued that the contest benefited only plastic surgeons and cosmetics manufacturers. Its TV audience for this year was one of the highest ever, at 2.2 billion viewers worldwide.

1997 Diana Hayden, India.

1998 Linor Abargil, Israel.

1999 Yukta Mookhey, India.

2000 Priyanka Chopra, India.

Organiser Eric Morley died at the beginning of November, weeks before the contest. His wife and co-organizer, Julia Morley, took control of the event and one of her first tasks after the title was awarded to Miss India was to issue the statement, 'there is no fixing in the Miss World beauty contest'. This was because of intense media speculation at the time over the dominance of India in the contest in recent years and the surge of multinational companies investing in the region. In the final round of questioning, Chopra had been asked to name the living woman she admired the most. She answered 'Mother Teresa', who had been dead for three years. The answer won her the crown but increased speculation of contest-rigging. Justifying her answer, Priyanka, who had previously revealed that she wanted to be a clinical psychologist so as 'to understand why people turn demented', said, 'For me she is a living legend. She does live on for me.'

2001 Agbani Darego, Nigeria.

2002 Azra Akın, Turkey.

Scheduled to take place in Abuja, Nigeria, the contest was boycotted by several nations in protest at the death sentence by stoning imposed by an Islamic Sharia court on Amina Lawal, a Nigerian woman who had been accused of adultery after having a child outside of marriage. Protests then erupted in Kaduna, Nigeria, after a Lagos-based journalist wrote that the Prophet Muhammad would have approved of the Miss World contest and might even have wanted to marry one of the competitors. Rioting left an estimated 220 dead, 1,200 injured, and 12,000 homeless. The contest was relocated to London, where the writer Muriel Gray said, 'These girls will be wearing swim wear dripping with blood.'

2003 Rosanna Davison, Ireland.

2004 María Julia Mantilla, Peru.

2005 Unnur Birna Vilhjálmsdóttir, Iceland.

The Miss World 1983 finalist, Unnur Steinsson of Iceland, was three months pregnant during the pageant. This violated the pageant's rules and ordinarily warranted disqualification; however, it wasn't discovered until after the pageant. Her baby, born on 25 May 1984, was the 2005 winner.

2006 Taťána Kuchařová, Czech Republic.

2007 Zhang Zilin, China.

2008 Ksenia Sukhinova, Russia.

Acknowledgements

To the many magnificent and strange advertisers of the LRB
personals column – thank you. You have refused to listen to any
dating advice other than mine for more than a decade and, as a
result, are probably doomed to wander the earth alone like love
zombies. I accept no responsibility whatsoever. I'd also like to
thank the business and editorial staff of the LRB for nurturing
such a committed audience. Belated thanks are due to Kate
Griffin at Profile for her Olympian work on the previous volume,
They Call Me Naughty Lola, and to Ginny Flynn for letting me
wear her clothes and make-up. At Scribner, I'm grateful to Nan
Graham and Susan Moldow for indulging this nonsense, to
Kate Bittman for indulging my constant whining and to Anna
deVries for lurking in the shadows with me to help fashion this
book from the lava and sediment of so many broken hearts
and dreams. To Nicola, Alannah, and Edith Rose, I owe far too
much to express here, but in the context of this book – thank
you for eating dinner while I banged on about how awesome
it would be to be put in a choke-hold by Phil Fondacaro. To my
unofficial biographer/priest and personal chef, Reverend Tim
Johnson, I'd like to offer my eternal gratitude for often cutting
short his evenings watching *The Real Ghostbusters* to volunteer
an unending stream of military aircraft trivia, which has served
me well in the making of this book and, indeed, my evolution
as a man. Thank you to Ramone's bakery and café in Eureka
and the Ya Habibi dance troupe in Arcata, California, for letting
me mooch from their wi-fi signals more times than I ever had
the guts to admit to. I'd especially like to thank the following
individuals, whose marks, wisdoms, and insights are firmly

impressed upon the LRB personals and the forgotten wishes of lonely people throughout the intellectual world: Laird Barrett, Howard Bromelow, Ben Campbell, Bryony Dalefield, Vera Huebner, Kate Parkinson, Louisa Sommerville, Nicholas Spice, and Sara Tsiringakis. But the biggest thank-you of all goes to Nina Stegeman, who waved her crooked wand and suffered far too many rewrites, far too much of my angst, and an excess of general bullshit so that this volume, and my literary reputation, could stake their rightful claim in bathrooms across the United States and beyond.

Index of lead-ins

Index of terms